A PRACTICAL GUIDE TO

THE
RUNES

The Runes: Simple Symbols, Rooted in Nature

The runes are simple, earthy symbols rooted in the natural world. If you look and are aware, you will can find runes everywhere—in the branches of trees, in cracks in the sidewalk, even in the graffiti scratched onto park benches. The more you allow the runes to be a part of your everyday life, the more comfortable you will be with them and the more they will speak to you of their inner meanings.

About the Author

Lisa Peschel is an artist, a writer and a Pagan of the Wiccan Tradition. She actively serves to educate the general public about this natural way of life in addition to divinatory practice and herbalism. She lives in North Carolina with her son Dylan MacLir.

To Write to the Author

If you wish to contact the author or would like more information about this book, please write to the author in care of Llewellyn Worldwide, and we will forward your request. Both the author and publisher appreciate hearing from you and learning of your enjoyment of this book and how it has helped you. Llewellyn Worldwide cannot guarantee that every letter written to the author can be answered, but all will be forwarded. Please write to:

Lisa Peschel
c/o Llewellyn Worldwide
P.O. Box 64383, Dept. L593-3,
St. Paul, MN 55164-0383, U.S.A.

Please enclose a self-addressed, stamped envelope for reply,or $1.00 to cover costs. If outside the U.S.A., enclose international postal reply coupon.

A PRACTICAL GUIDE TO
THE RUNES

Their Uses in Divination and Magick

LISA PESCHEL

2003
Llewellyn Publications
St. Paul, Minnesota, 55164-0383, U.S.A.

FIRST EDITION, 1989
Eleventh printing, 2003
Cover Design: Gavin Dayton Duffy
Interiors by Lisa Peschel and Christopher Wells

Library of Congress Cataloging-in-Publication Data
Peschel, Lisa, 1961-
    A practical guide to the runes.

    (Llewellyn's new age series)
    Bibliography: p.
    1. Fortune-telling by runes. 2. Runes—Miscellanea.
I. Title. II. Series.
BF1891.R85P47   1989   133.4   89-2246
ISBN 0-87542-593-3

Llewellyn Publications
A Division of Llewellyn Worldwide, Ltd.
P.O. 64383, St. Paul, MN 55164-0383
http://www.llewellyn.com

Printed in the United States of America

This book is dedicated with love and gratitude to Cal and Becky Neal, without whose support and caring above and beyond the call of duty, it could never have seen print at all, and most especially to my son Dylan MacLir, who made it all possible.

CONTENTS

Introduction 1

1. Tools of the Trade 13
   Your Runes
   The Rune Pouch
   The Rune Cloth

2. The Runes in Divination 27

3. Principles of Divination and Rune Layouts 97
   The One-Rune Method
   The Three-Rune Method
   The Five-Rune Method
   The Seven-Rune Method

4. The Runes in Magick 117

5. Principles of Rune Magick 129

6. Talismans 135
   Runescripts
   Bindrunes

7. Ritual Carving and Consecration 151

Appendices 163

Suggested Reading List 171

INTRODUCTION

The runic system was in use by the Nordic and Germanic tribes of Northern Europe for both secular and religious purposes. There is some debate among scholars, but the first examples of the runes to phonetically represent language appear to date from around the second century B.C.E. The development of the rune alphabet was a fairly recent occurrence, brought about by the increased trading activity with Mediterranean neighbors who already possessed a fully developed alphabet.

Before this time, the runes were primarily a magickal system of pictographs representing the forces and objects in Nature. It was believed that by calling upon the appropriate rune one could thereby make contact with the force in Nature the symbol represented.

There were several different runic alphabets in use throughout Northern Europe over the centuries, but the most common is the Germanic or Elder FUTHARK. This alphabet received its name from its first six letters—F, U, TH, A, R and K. It was the system most widely in use between 200 B.C.E. and the late eighth century and the one we shall be concerned with in this book. This alphabet contains 24 letters and is divided up into three groups of eight called Freya's Eight, Hagall's Eight, and Tir's Eight.

What you have here is a book about runic divination and magick. You will find little information on the actual history, customs, or mythology of the Norse and Anglo-Saxon peoples who used these runes contained herein. There have been many excellent books on these subjects written by scholars from all over the world, and in this work I have chosen to focus on the practical aspect of the runes rather than the historical.

This is not to slight the importance of a basic knowledge of these subjects. It is as important to understand the physical and mental realities of those who created the runes as it is to understand the meanings of the individual runes themselves. For what are the runes if not a magickal extension of the experiences and realities of the Northern European? You will find in the suggested reading list at the back of this book several fine works covering these areas, and I urge you to check them out.

The aim of this book is to get as much useful runic information in one place as possible. This is primarily for the benefit of the novice. Until I began compiling the notes that were to become this book, I would use up to five different sources in my quest to discover the most accurate interpretation of the runecast.

As can be expected from such disorganized behavior, sometimes an answer would be realized and sometimes not. Flipping through reams of information is not conducive in the least bit to gaining a true inner meaning of the runes in question. This was the period in my runic development in which I learned that you cannot accurately divine from a book. Not this book, not any book. Books are simply tools to help us get started and to stimulate our minds to seek further and learn for ourselves.

It is truly unfortunate for our studies that we are born in the twentieth century instead of, say, the sixth. Were we living in the sixth century we could have been taught orally by our village shaman. The shaman was the high priest and magician of his people. To him fell the responsibility of making certain all the crops grew, the hunts were successful and the women were fertile. He also held the mysteries of the runes. With the runes he could bless and curse, hurt and heal. He could also divine, and it was for this ability that he was much in demand by all, chieftains and peasants alike.

It must be remembered that the runes were MYSTERIES to these people, in every sense of the word. They were FORCES, secret allies that the knowledgeable could use for many purposes. Their magickal use was entrusted to the

A composite drawing of Fachwerk elements commonly used in buildings across Europe, especially Germany and France. Runes to look for in this picture include Eolh, Wunjo, Isa, Tir, Gifu, Ing, Ansuz and Hagall.

very few, and the knowledge was never written down for the eyes of the (perhaps) unworthy. All information was transmitted by mouth and learned by heart. Through diligent study and proper use, the runes could help you become closer to the gods and aid you in ordinary day-to-day living.

There were runes to influence the weather, to aid the crops and to heal the sick. Runes were carved on many items. Weapons, drinking horns, spears, the prows of ships and the timbers of the houses—each had its own combination of runes, usually for luck and protection.

The runes were an important part of the lives of these people, and they drew a certain comfort from seeing their powerful symbols on even the homeliest of objects.

In fact, what we call the Tudor or half-timbered building style has evolved from the Germanic *Fachwerk* (half-timbered) architecture. The placing of the timbers at angles in the plaster was originally done in such a way as to form a specific rune shape. This shape was then believed to impart its power and magickal significance to the building itself with the building passing it on to the people living inside. Although the architects of today do not concern themselves with the magickal qualities of their structures, it is still possible to discern some runes in the timbers of modern homes. This is a fun thing to do if you happen to pass such a house, and it is also a good exercise in familiarizing yourself with the rune symbols.

You will find that if you look and are aware you can find runes everywhere—in the branches of trees, in cracks in the sidewalk, even in the graffiti scratched onto park benches. The more you allow the runes to be a part of your everyday life, the more comfortable you will be with them and the more they will speak to you of their inner meanings.

It was this familiarity that allowed the rune-using peoples to tap their power so effectively. Like their northern gods, the runes permeated the culture of the Norse peoples and were an important force in their lives.

Unfortunately, we do not have village magicians today, and we must rely upon books. Even the fortunate few of you who will be able to one day receive personalized instruction from a runic magician must realize that even your teacher's knowledge came either directly or indirectly from books. Some of these books, naturally, are better than others. What raises these really fine books above the rest is the quality of personal insight that the authors were able to bring to the work.

This *quality of personal insight* is also what raises one runic magician above another and is one of the most important points I have to make in this book. Of course, we in this century must recourse to books for our basic knowledge. There's no disputing that. But what do we do with that knowledge once we have it? Simply proceeding in a copycat manner and parroting memorized material is not enough. We must *think!* We must take that basic information and transmute it, like an alchemist of old, turning the lead of rote information into the gold of true knowledge via the element of our personal life experiences.

A rune, like any other ideograph, is merely a frozen symbol of an actual state or concept. What these symbols mean can change radically, depending on the perspective of the interpreter. Through continued use of the runes and through meditation on each symbol, one can draw within and gain a truer picture of the symbols as they relate to one's own life.

Some authors have theorized that individuals of Northern European descent are more naturally attuned to the symbolism of the runes than those who are not. Certainly there is some truth in this, but it is this attitude of racial superiority which led to the debased use of the runes and pre-runic symbols, such as the swastika, by some inner circles of the Nazi regime. For a long time, this association colored the impressions ordinary people had of runic studies.

There is no doubt that some people will be more adept at using the runes than others, but with study and careful thought, anyone can learn to use this system. The runes are simple, earthy symbols rooted in the natural world and as such can be touched and related to by anyone who is willing to ally themselves with those forces which make up our natural world. Some of these forces are old and familiar friends. As Marijane Osborne and Stella Longland wrote in their excellent book

Rune Games:

   "Other divination systems such as the Tarot,
I Ching, etc., although excellent in themselves,
tend to split the Northern European intellect off
from its physical experience because they are not
indigenous to its cultural environment. For example, if we have lived near oak trees but not near
palms and pomegranates, we have a physical
appreciation of the oak tree as a symbol in the
runes in a way that we cannot have a physical
appreciation of the palm or the pomegranate as
they appear on the High Priestess card of the
Rider deck. If we have never experienced a palm
tree in its environment, we can appreciate its
symbolism (only) intellectually, whereas we can
appreciate an oak tree both physically and intellectually."

   We each have our own personal experiences
of those things, such as an oak tree, cattle, hail,
ice, the Sun, etc., depicted in the runes. It is up to
each of us to discover a personal runic interpretation for these things, for only by doing so can we
utilize the full potential of the rune system. These
interpretations can be discovered and worked
out through dreams, significant events, or anything else that stimulates the subconscious, such
as meditation. Once these interpretations are
learned, they can be utilized through magick and
divination, stimulating your individual imagination and helping you perceive your relationship

to the world around you in a different way, thus enabling you to effect changes in your future.

However, the runes should never be allowed to entirely dictate your actions. Their purpose is to be a tool for discovering your magickal identity as well as your personal creative archetypal symbols so that you can draw within to find the solutions to your dilemmas. The ability to determine the future lies not with the symbols themselves but in the *mind* that uses them.

The runes are there to guide you through your problems by showing you what is LIKELY to happen, giving you variables, and suggesting how you should behave if the event comes to pass. Like an astrological chart, a runecast is a map of something that is likely to happen given your orientation in the world at the time of the inquiry. It is not an absolute. There is no reason why you should resign yourself to disaster every time your runecast indicates a problem. Sure, you could be a fatalist and make funeral arrangements because a reading indicated the high probability of an accident on your next big road trip, but you could also say "Aha!," take charge, examine the variables and find a solution. If it really looked that bad, you could always postpone the trip until the next convenient time. Knowledge is power!! Don't automatically resign yourself to Fate. Using your runic foresight, grab hold of Fate and wrestle it onto the path that you desire.

That's what the runes are all about. Helping

you take charge of your life. Face it, you would not have purchased this book if you didn't think that it would help you to improve your life situation. So don't waste your money and don't waste the knowledge by blindly surrendering yourself to Fate. Our forefathers left us a great legacy in these powerful symbols that we in the '80s are only now truly beginning to grasp. Let's not insult their memory by a slipshod use of their gift.

Please remember that the runes should never be used as a means of making a quick buck or treated like an amusing Ouija board parlor game. As a human being, you perform best when treated with plenty of respect, and the runes do as well.

When you pick up this book and the set of runes which you will make, you are an inheritor of one of the greatest and most noble paths—that of the runic magician. It is a path of great responsibility as well as great power. Study hard and always listen to your inner voice. Allow it to speak within you, and follow its lead, whether it agrees with your books or not. Never allow a book (or a person, for that matter) to feed you absolutes. I doubt the sincerity of any book or form of instruction that says "If you don't do exactly as I tell you, the gods will be angry and the sky will fall down." Any person or course of study that leaves no room for personal insight and individual perception is merely indulging its own ego. Find your own path, and make your own way. In our hectic and trauma-filled world, it is so much easier to let others lead us around by the nose. There is no room for that when dealing with the runes, for they encourage us to explore the worlds and to question. Be ever mindful of the law of karma, for anything you put out, be it positive or negative, will reflect back to you like light off a mirror, often with a kick.

It must be stressed that the runic lore is "open ended." That is to say, books can give you only the basics; they can't give you the whole picture. For the talented and studious individual, there is no limit to the applications that can be found once a basic and personal understanding of each rune as it relates to the natural world and its neighbors is realized.

The runic path is one that has brought nothing but good into my life, and if you pursue it with equal enthusiasm, it will benefit you as well.

TOOLS OF THE TRADE

Your Runes

The runes that you are about to make will be valuable allies in your journey through life. It is good to view them as friends. Always treat them with respect, and as you craft your rune set, craft each and every one with love.

Do not lend your runes out to anyone. They are for your own personal use. By the time you have finished crafting them you will have imbued them with YOUR energy and YOUR life force, and they were made to serve YOUR purposes. Some people don't even like to do readings for anybody else, but I don't think that the small amount of time they will be in the hands of another for divinatory purposes will alter the bond which you have created with them. Again, this is strictly a matter of personal preference, and you will have to decide how you feel about it.

Sometimes you may find that all of the people you know (and some that you don't know)

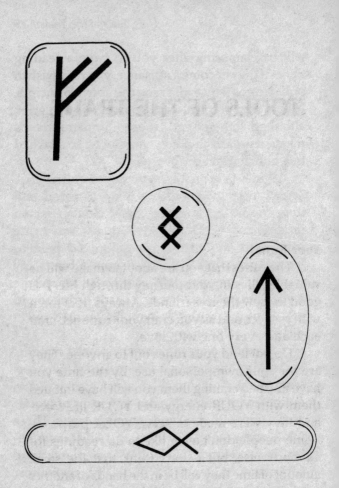

Rune Shapes and Sizes

Figure 1

will be clamoring after you to have a reading done. If they become a nuisance, you may wish to put a stop to it by explaining the above principle. In this way you will save yourself a lot of grief, although some of your more mundane friends may not understand how you can be so attached to a bunch of pieces of wood!

Runes can be made from any natural material. They can be made of stone, clay, or wood, and they should be made by hand by the person intending to use them. My first set was made from fairly uniform stream-smoothed pebbles from Japan which I scooped from a bin at my local Pier One imports store. These served me well. The set I have now I made from round pieces of oak with the symbols painted on in red.

Wood has long been the preferred material for making the runes, which explains why sets from the early centuries have not survived to enlighten us today. Words for "pieces of wood" associated with the runes are numerous. Three Old Norse examples of this are STAFR (stave, letter, or secret lore), TEINN (twig, talismanic word for divination), and HLUTR (lot for divination, talismanic object).

The oldest rune pieces in existence are etched on bone. I suppose you could also use bone to make your runes, but while I have no doubt they would be very beautiful, I feel that the life force of the animal is still too much a part of the bone material to make the runes conducive to the vibrations of the individual symbols painted on them. No matter how well-bleached, they are still permeated with the energies of death, and I would never use them.

The Latin writer Tacitus tells us that the Germanic tribes cast lots using strips of fruitwood inscribed with symbols. A later source states that the strips were crafted from ash. Whatever wood is used, it is important that the wood have a personal meaning for the individual who will eventually be using the set. This can be a decision based on the knowledge of the magickal properties of the tree involved, or it can simply be a tree which brings back happy memories from one's childhood.

Figure 1 illustrates some suggested rune shapes and sizes. When choosing the shape and size of your runes, be sure to keep in mind that all 25 should be able to fit in the palms of your cupped hands. Good dimensions for this are a length of no more than 4 cm, a width of no more than 3 cm, and a thickness of no more than 1 cm.

Round runes are perhaps the easiest to make. If you wish, you can collect the wood for your runes from the wild. Find the tree of your choice and collect from it a branch about ¾" in diameter. Remember, if you take live wood, you are taking the equivalent of a finger from a living being, and respectfully ask the tree's permission before cutting it anywhere. Explain to the tree the use of the wood, and thank the tree after you have finished.

Some people also bury a silver (or silver-colored) coin at the base of the trunk as payment and in thanks.

Cut the branch into 25 pieces approximately 1 cm thick. The bark can be left on or taken off. An easier way to get uniform round pieces is to go to a good hardware store and purchase a dowel made from the wood of your choice. You will not have as wide a selection this way, but you should be able to choose from a few types. Pine, oak, and ash are all likely types of wood to be found in a dowel.

The rune symbols themselves can either be carved into the wood, painted on, or drawn on with a felt-tip pen. I prefer the carved and painted methods because these methods require more effort, and the more effort you put into your rune set, the more you will get out of it. My runes were painted on using a small sable brush and acrylic paint. Acrylic paints are really ideal, being easy to clean up after, durable and bright. However, if you really feel so inept with a paintbrush that you cannot bring yourself to use one, there are a number of companies which produce a paint marker. These markers come in any number of vivid colors and are as easy to use as a regular felt-tip pen.

I have mixed feelings about the use of stains on wooden runes. Any stain used should not be too many shades darker than the natural wood, and it should, of course, be applied before the runic symbol is painted. Depending on the type of stains and paints used, the color of the stain can change the essential color of the overlying paint. This is the primary objection I have to stains. However, in this as well as in all other runic matters, use your own intuition regarding what is right for you.

Sealants I am definitely against. Varnish and shellac will seal all the pores in the wood and give the rune an unnatural sheen, but more importantly, it will preclude any actual touching of the natural wood surface. This will seal off any energies the wood possesses, and in my opinion, if you are going to varnish your runes, you might just as well make them out of plastic.

Be sure that when you choose your runes there are no identifying marks on the reverse sides. This insures that when the runes are turned face down for selection a biased selection cannot be made. For this reason, it is unwise to decorate the back side in any way unless your runes are round, in which case it is useful to paint a simple line on the back indicating the North/South axis of the rune.

After you have gathered all of your tools and materials together to start crafting your runes, take a moment of quiet time. In this moment, still your mind and concentrate on what you are about to do. You are about to reach back in time, continuing an ancient tradition. You are about to craft for yourself a set of tools that will help you to get in touch with and be more in control of the natural world. You are building friends. Taking this quiet time to meditate on the task at hand or to pray to your individual gods elevates a simple woodshop project to the level of a ritual.

You may have observed that I have used the word *gods* several times in this book. Whether you are Pagan or Christian, whether you worship one god or many, you can still use the runes. However, whatever your faith, it is important to realize and accept that the runes and the runic system, as well as the entire reality of the Norse peoples, accepted the existence of many gods and forces as a matter of course. These gods and their influence inundated the lives of these rune-using people and should not be ignored by the runic student, whatever his personal religious feelings. The efficiency of the system presented herein can only be increased by a thorough understanding of the Norse peoples, their gods, and the special place that runes held in their society. Through this understanding (and notice I say *understanding* and not knowledge, for you can have plenty of knowledge and still not understand), you can gain a feel for the atmosphere in which the rune lore was first practiced, and from a true understanding you can only benefit.

Traditionally, Odin and Freya were the guardians and patrons of the runes, and many runic practitioners still pray to them for aid and knowledge. If you are Christian, you can imagine Odin as Jehovah, since that is his status in the Norse pantheon, and you can imagine Freya to be that principle of light and growth which is embodied so beautifully in the bursting out of spring. For we are all striving to understand the will of our gods through the runes while aiming for personal growth, both in the material and spiritual worlds.

In our study of the runes both as a form of divination and as tools for magickal change, we would do well to keep in mind the fact that the conversion from the Pagan ways to the new Christian faith took far longer than most historians would have us believe. It was certainly not a case of waving a magick wand with everybody becoming Christian overnight. Whereas the ruling classes may have spotted the political benefits to be gained from conversion (or feigned conversion), the peasants, who were the backbone of the culture as well as the majority of it, held fast to their own beliefs and steadfastly refused to conform to the new religion. The Pagan faith lingered on longest in Iceland, where most of the population remained with the Old Faith until well into the eleventh century. Even today there is a thriving, openly Pagan community there, and it is there that a living tradition of the runes survives to this very day.

So take your quiet time. Concentrate on what you hope to accomplish. Call upon Odin and Freya, if you wish, to guide your hands and help you over any difficulties in the creation of your new runes. Perhaps you are not familiar with any sort of woodworking or are afraid of making a mistake while painting on the symbols. Don't fret.

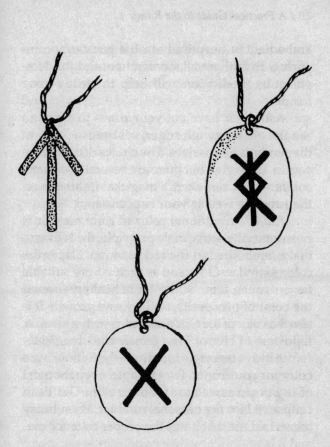

The ways in which runes can be used in jewelry are limited only by your skill and imagination. Soapstone is an excellent material for jewelry, being readily available and easily worked. Other possibilities are wood, bone, and metal. The little unengraved metal pendant disks one can sometimes get at fairs are excellent and can be painted on with ease, and the paint can also be removed with ease in case of error.

You would be surprised at what you can accomplish with faith and concentration, and this simple quiet meditation will help to steady your hand.

After you have cut your runes to size and sanded off any rough edges, it is time to paint on the symbols themselves. The choice of color is, of course, up to you, but there are several traditional colors which can exert a magickal influence on the runes as well as your subconscious.

Red is a traditional color of rune magick. It represents the active male principle, the life force that is embodied in the red of blood. *Blue* is the color sacred to Odin and as such is very suitable for the runes. It is also a color of healing. *Green* is the color of prosperity, fertility, and growth. It is also the color of the Goddess and as such is ideal for followers of Her or for a female rune magician.

Always use your intuition when choosing a color for your runes. For example, even though I am a woman as well as a follower of the Goddess, I chose red for my personal rune set. My subconscious told me that it was the proper color for me.

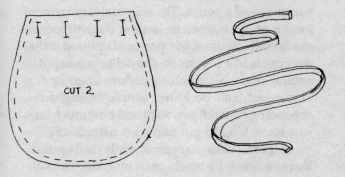

Leather Pouch

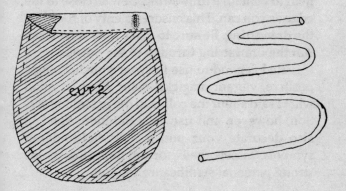

Fabric Pouch
Figure 2

The Rune Pouch

In order to insure that none of your runes becomes lost and to simplify transporting them, you will need a pouch. The only real requirement for this pouch is that it be large enough to accommodate all 25 runes. My personal opinion is that the pouch, like the runes, should be made out of natural materials, such as cotton, linen or fur. This pouch can be either simple or elaborate, depending on what you want and how much time you are willing to put into its construction.

Figure 2 shows a typical, easily made pouch. You can sew it by machine or by hand. The simplest pouch can be made of leather with vertical slits at the top to allow a thong or cord to be passed through and drawn tight. If you make a cloth pouch, allow an extra inch at the top. This allows you to turn over the edge and make a ½" hem to contain a drawstring. Sew as close to the edge as you can. This ensures plenty of room for the drawstring. Be sure to make a slit so you can run the drawstring through to the outside.

Red is good to use for your pouch, being a positive, vibrant magickal color. Keep in mind what I said about the colors in the preceding section, however, and use your intuition. You can also decorate your pouch with embroidered symbols, tassels, bells, or anything that holds strong personal significance for you.

The Rune Cloth

Once again, we can look to Tacitus for insight

into the methods of the rune magicians. In Chapter 10 of *Germania,* he states that after crafting the rune pieces from the fruitwood they are scattered at random on a white cloth.

White is the symbol of *truth* and *purity* and as such is ideal for use in the rune cloth. It also has the advantage of being *totally neutral visually.* That is the most important thing to consider when making your rune cloth. No matter what color you choose for your cloth, it should be free of visual distractions. It should not be a print, and it should not be highly ornamented as these things can distract the mind and lead the eye away from the runes themselves.

The material for this cloth can easily be obtained from the remnant table of your local fabric emporium. A good median size is 18″ × 18″.

The main purpose of this cloth is to keep the runes clean and to provide a focus for the rune layout itself.

In order to charge your runes—that is, to imprint them with your own personal vibrations—it is recommended that your runes be in contact with your person as often as possible. They can be worn at the belt, carried in the purse, or held in the lap as you watch TV. Try to position the pouch on your solar plexus region. This is the space approximately between your diaphragm and your navel. This area is known to be an energy center, and your personal aura is strongly felt there. You can also place it beneath your pillow before you go to sleep. You may find that this method will also bring you the added benefit of significant dreams, often on runic themes.

Your runes do not have to be in contact with you at all times, of course, but the point is that an effort must be made to attune the runes to your own personal "wavelength" before any serious attempt at actual divination is made.

THE RUNES
IN DIVINATION

The information in this section deals with the individual runes and the way they behave in divination.

It is crucial for an accurate interpretation that you familiarize yourself very thoroughly with each rune and learn how each interacts with its neighbors. This latter information cannot be immediately grasped, but rather it must be learned through meditation and your widening experiences with divination. It is not an instant science, but one which, if pursued, will bring you much peace of mind and satisfaction.

I have attempted to help by including in each explanation those runes which are particularly significant when placed near the rune in question. Of course, there are many more correspondences than those which I have listed here, and you should try to keep a notebook handy for those times when you may get a sudden insight into a rune's particular meaning. Write it down, or else you're liable to forget it. Keeping notes on each divination can also be illuminating, especially when you are able to see those events come to pass that were foretold weeks or months earlier. A notebook like this can be a very reassuring symbol of both your progress and the honesty of the runes.

With these clues and much study, it should not be long before you gain a much truer understanding of how the runes act in the divination process and are able to use this knowledge to help you in your life, as well as in the lives of all who may turn to you for a runecast.

Reading for other people is a heavy responsibility and should not be undertaken lightly. It is much more important to be accurate when you interpret for others than it is when you interpret for yourself. It is often more difficult, for you do not have that inner understanding of them and their problems that you are privy to in readings for yourself. If you misread your personal runecast, at least you are fully aware of your own interpretive shortcomings. Usually when people reach the stage where their problem is so troubling that they recourse to divination, they are in a total state of helpless confusion and are ready to accept anything you may prophesy as gospel.

Giving these poor troubled people biased or inaccurate information at this time is akin to taking advantage of someone who is handicapped. Wrong information could be disastrous to them.

You are also in danger when reading for

another. Playing "Dear Abby" or deliberately telling the querent what you think s/he wants to hear is not just "comforting a friend." It is the most heinous type of white lie and is sure to cause you to incur negative karma. And believe me, paying back karmic debts is never an entertaining prospect.

Read this section thoroughly, ask the Forces for guidance, and remember to practice on yourself before you even consider casting for another.

The runes are powerful forces, and through proper use can enlighten and aid you along life's thorny paths. Use them wisely.

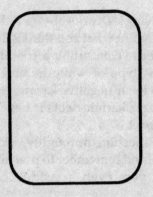

WYRD

The blank rune, known as **WYRD**, is a totally modern addition to the Futhark system, although the concept it represents was certainly well known to the rune-using peoples.

It takes its name from the Norse *Wyrd* (pronounced "weird"), the collective term for the three Norse sisters known as the Norns. Individually known as Urdhr, Verthandi, and Skuld— past, present, and future, respectively—they represented All Knowledge and were special patrons of the art of divination.

I do not know when this rune was first conceived, but my first exposure to it was in the pioneering *Book of Runes* by Ralph Blum. He refers to it as Odin and states: "This is a rune of total trust and should be taken as exciting evidence of your most immediate contact with your own true destiny." *WYRD is the cosmic power of Fate.*

It is closely akin to the idea expressed by the Sanskrit word *karma*—that we ourselves must accept the responsibility for our own actions, be they good or bad. When this rune appears in your reading, you may be certain that something unexpected is going to come to you. Whether this something is positive or negative depends on what you warrant by virtue of your past behavior.

WYRD has no number and no pictographic symbol with which to clue us in on its meaning in the reading. Its meaning can best be interpreted by the way in which it relates to its neighbors.

Having no number and no symbol makes WYRD, in effect, a *non*-rune. The concept expressed by it is neither concrete nor of this world. WYRD operates through a completely separate dimension than that of the other runes and can often indicate that the matter in question is "in the lap of the gods."

A useful way to view WYRD, especially in meditation, is as a *void*. When you see its blank surface appear, envision it as a hole—a gateway to another dimension—in which there is both Everything and Nothing. Through this rune will the voices of the gods invariably be made manifest, although very often their voices are communicated through the Inner ear.

WYRD shows that which is destined to be and cannot be avoided. Being so ambiguous, it can as easily mean a bad occurrence as a good one.

When this rune appears in a prominent place in your runecast, it indicates that should a certain step be taken life may never again be the same for you. Drawing it can often be frightening, for do we not fear the most what we understand the least? Trust in yourself and in the gods.

WYRD does not always represent something negative or fateful, but it usually does represent things that are at present hidden from view. Sometimes this can be a secret or something that must remain undisclosed for your own good. In a runecast in which information about another person is the primary point of inquiry, the appearance of this rune can signify that you are seeking information which you have no right to know.

Always look to the runes around WYRD for any clue as to its meaning, especially the ones immediately following it and the rune that occupies the result position.

For instance, if WYRD were to fall with GIFU or another love rune, it could indicate a wonderful new relationship that will be coming into your life, perhaps as a reward for actions well-done in the past.

When WYRD falls in the result position, it often shows that a simple resolution to the problem in question is either not available to you at this time or totally in the hands of Fate.

All in all, WYRD is a very complex concept that will mean different things to different people. We each have our own idea of the manner in which the forces of Fate move in our lives, and it is this personal perception which must be fully understood before WYRD's location in a reading can be truly and accurately interpreted.

FEHU

To the Northern Europeans, this rune meant *cattle*. In archaic times, cattle were the measure of a man's worth. They gave him status within his tribe, and they kept him and his family alive. Through hard work and careful husbandry, his herds would prosper, calves would appear, and he became richer.

As time went on and cultural behaviors changed, gold and other materials replaced cattle as the primary indicators of wealth, but the rune of **FEHU** remained a symbol of earned income—something which has to be worked for but will produce an expected source of revenue.

Along with OTHEL, FEHU is a rune of *material gain*. When upright, it usually indicates prosperity coming to you in some form.

This is a rune of *fulfillment*—something which

you have been striving toward will finally be within your grasp. It signifies overcoming opposition, whether personal (another individual thwarting your plans) or impersonal (a bad situation, time frame, etc.). When FEHU is upright, especially in the result position, it suggests that you have what it takes to win out over the opposing forces through diligence and hard work.

Look to the other runes with which FEHU is paired for other clues to its meaning. Paired with love runes, it can signify a romantic gain of some sort. It suggests that any declaration of tender feelings will be well received, if only you can get up the courage to express them.

It can also indicate a fortunate new career opportunity or, because of its association with something earned, a fortunate financial investment.

If FEHU is surrounded by negative or delaying runes, it may signify that the time is not right for any new beginnings which you may be contemplating, either in romance, such as starting a new love affair, or in business, as in a new partnership or agreement.

In this case, you would best be advised to concentrate on hoarding or conserving what you already have gained, rather than jumping with both feet into totally uncharted territory.

If the question deals with whether or not you should drop one project in favor of another, FEHU's counsel is to keep on with the task. As long as this rune remains upright, no matter how difficult things may seem at present, one should not give up while there is still even the remotest chance of success. You may be experiencing bad times now, but the dawn always follows the dark. With FEHU, you are put on notice that it is almost sunrise.

Reversed: Reversed, FEHU indicates a loss or disappointment of some sort if you continue on in the same manner.

When the surrounding runes are essentially positive, it may merely be a disappointing delay, an obstacle in your path that you would prefer not to deal with at this time.

In a primarily negative runecast, it could indicate a material loss which cannot be recovered. Also, it may counsel you to abandon any plan already under way as it is not likely to prove very effective in the long run.

You may be experiencing considerable frustration in your life at the moment. This is a time when you will have a lot of problems maintaining your financial or emotional status.

When FEHU reversed relates to romantic involvement, it indicates that possible arguments, doubts, and suspicions may arise, but unless surrounded by truly negative runes, the problem may only be temporary.

Whenever this rune comes up reversed, be especially vigilant. Doubtful situations are everywhere, and care must be taken not to become entangled at this time in any deals or relationships which could bring grief later on.

URUZ

URUZ is the rune of the Aurochs, or *wild ox*, and in many ways is akin to FEHU. However, FEHU represents the domesticated, predictable farm cattle, whereas URUZ represents the vital, wild force and energy of the hardy wild ox that ranged over the same territory and was so much a part of the life of the Northern Tribes.

This wild bison symbolized strength and virility to these people, hence URUZ is considered to be a powerful indicator of *good health and strong natural powers of resistance*. Whenever this rune arises where health is an issue, it indicates a speedy recovery from the illness or affliction in question.

URUZ can sometimes indicate the *male* in any relationship and signifies *strong emotions*. It can also represent the *True Will* of the querent—

that thing which he truly desires. Depending on the surrounding runes, it will very probably come to pass. This is a forceful, driving, masculine rune.

This rune rules over *changes*, usually those of a sudden or unexpected kind that compel you to draw within yourself to utilize that force of honest, raw strength that only this rune can supply.

These changes are often natural ones and should not be avoided. We must remember that like a snake shedding its skin it is often necessary for us to peel away the old to make way for the new. Examine those things in your life which you may be overly attached to at this time. Look to the runes around URUZ—you may be called upon to give up these things.

In questions of business or finance, this rune indicates an eventual improvement but only through diligent application of your resources and much effort. URUZ often appears in a rune-cast to herald a promotion or a new career, usually with added responsibilities. In this case, the appearance of URUZ assures you that whatever the new burden you will undeniably have the strength to deal with it. It is a rune of raw, archetypal force.

Paired with positive runes, it indicates good fortune and certain success, whatever the assumed odds.

Reversed: URUZ here shows that you are about to fail or have already failed to take advantage of the moment. Search your memories. Have you passed up a good opportunity because of petty worries? Have you allowed fear and a low self-image to hold you back?

Sometimes this rune can indicate weak will power. This can manifest as a lack of motivation or as a desire to let someone else, someone you may view as a "stronger individual," dictate your beliefs and tell you how to live your life. It might even seem as though your strength is being used against you at this time. This is especially indicated when GIFU or WUNJO is in close proximity in the reading.

As this is a primary rune of health, URUZ reversed can show low vitality or a minor illness that will soon have to be faced. For a male, it can also suggest problems, whether psychological or physiological, of a sexual nature.

Even reversed, URUZ can still indicate surprise changes in your life. If it falls with change runes, such as EHWAZ or RAIDHO, it can show that your lack of motivation will lead you to pass by what will probably be a fortuitous change for the better.

If the tone of the reading is mainly negative, however, then URUZ indicates that you should let this change pass you by for it will only bring you trouble.

Reversed, as when upright, URUZ can herald a major change, although when this rune is reversed it signifies a change which you will not like very much. Things may yet turn out for the best though, especially if URUZ reversed falls in an otherwise positive runecast.

THURISAZ

THURISAZ is not only the vexing thorn which its name implies but also the glyph of the Hammer of Thor—the mighty weapon Mjollnir, protector of men and gods alike.

This rune has many associations with *protection* and with *luck*, especially if it is paired with EIHWAZ or EOLH. Sometimes this may herald a stroke of unexpected good luck, usually from an equally unexpected source rather than from someone you already know. You will be "in the right place at the right time" and reap the benefits.

On occasion, however, THURISAZ may appear in the runecast to indicate that the run of good luck you have been experiencing is about to come to an end. Take care not to collapse yourself too far into your own self-assuredness, for at this time you may receive a rude awakening.

Take stock of your situation and evaluate where you really stand before recklessly plunging onward.

In a case like this, it can show that you are being wrong-minded or stubborn in some way. The result which you have set your heart upon may not be so easily attainable because of your "I'm right, you're wrong" mindset. The runes surrounding THURISAZ will tell you whether this is in regard to business, finance or emotional relationships. If THURISAZ is found with HAGALL, NIED or ISA, you would do well to postpone any endeavor for the duration of the runecast's time frame, and if you are called upon to make a decision, be sure to consult with persons wiser and more impartial than yourself. This is especially necessary if this rune falls near ANSUZ, JERA or MANNAZ.

In short, if THURISAZ's negative aspects are in evidence, it usually means that you are being opposed by people who are either morally, politically, or financially stronger than yourself. This situation may or may not last, depending on the helpfulness of the surrounding runes.

In a strongly positive runecast, however, THURISAZ can indicate that powerful forces for protection, luck, and good health are entering your sphere at this time.

Reversed: THURISAZ reversed indicates much the same thing as it does upright. The main difference here is that either you or the individual you are reading for will not wish to heed the advice and information offered. You are set on this course of action and are very full of yourself, unwilling to accept any advice which is not generated from your brain and your experience.

When this rune is reversed, the consequences of blindly following your own path are even worse than they are when the rune is right side up.

It presages a time when your luck runs out, and you will need to muster much caution and act with circumspection regarding your situation at present. Any hasty decision is bound to cause regrets since it is brought about through a weakness in yourself. You will deceive even yourself about your motives at this time, and continuing on in this fashion will only create new problems, ones far more severe than the ones acting on your life at present.

Sometimes THURISAZ reversed indicates that you feel threatened by an individual that you perceive as weaker or subordinate to you in some sense. Look for the rune KENAZ reversed in the reading as a signal that this person is about to come to the forefront.

ANSUZ

The meaning of this rune is *mouth*, and as such usually indicates the *spoken word*, the *taking of advice*, or the *acquisition of wisdom*.

It can also indicate an *exam* of some sort, be it written (like a scholastic test) or oral (such as a job interview). When **ANSUZ** is found upright, however, fears should be put aside, for it indicates the ability to sail through whatever arises with eloquence and ease.

When you see this rune upright, be on the lookout during any meetings or chance encounters, especially those with older people or those wiser than yourself.

It denotes a need for careful thought and deliberation, often coupled with the advice of another. This advice may come from a parent or parental figure wise in the ways of the world and

43

the spirit. Heed it, for ANSUZ indicates open, unbiased advice that is honest and often helpful.

This advice, freely given and totally free of guile, may be just what you need to hear at this time in order to solve your dilemma. Look to the runes surrounding ANSUZ for a clue as to where your advice may originate. If the rune is BEORC, it will come from a close relative such as a mother or child—someone in your immediate family. OTHEL is an older relative, and JERA is likely to be a lawyer or some official type.

On occasion, this rune appears to suggest an apprenticeship to a new trade or refers to an aspect of life or a situation that you may never have encountered before. In this case, it is likely that you will be helped and guided by a sympathetic and patient individual who is attentive and knowledgeable from whom you will learn a great deal.

Reversed: Here ANSUZ shows lies, trickery, and general deceit. Don't believe anything you hear at this time, and take care to get a second opinion whenever you are in doubt.

Watch out! Someone else wants what's best for him or her, not what's best for you. This rune reversed indicates selfish, biased advice, often from an individual who is so enmeshed in the problem at hand that impartiality is lacking.

Parents or superiors may be trying to interfere with your plans at this time. You may feel concerned because of difficulties that inhibit you from accepting what is offered. There may appear to be failed communication and a lack of clarity in your past or present dilemma.

Drawing this rune reversed can indicate a failure or an outright refusal on your part to learn from life's lessons. It can also mean troubles with a course of study or a misuse of knowledge. Note the position of WYRD in relation to this. If it appears with other negative runes, it can show an eternal student, one who goes on accumulating knowledge for knowledge's sake while never really using it or intending to use it for any constructive purpose.

RAIDHO

The Nordic peoples identified this rune with the *wagon*, and as may be expected, it is a prime indicator of *travel* or *movement*.

RAIDHO is a symbol of travel, usually for pleasure. Taken in this sense, it will often show a safe or pleasant journey, usually without mishaps and often with convivial traveling companions.

Sometimes this journey can be an allegorical one, a journey of the soul. If this is the meaning that applies to you, now is the time to make that journey within. If you are already following your soul's path, this rune counsels you to keep on it.

RAIDHO also can indicate that now is a good time to enter into any discussions or negotiations. At this time, you are passing into a period conducive to logical thought and strategy. In all questions dealing with a difference of opinion, it suggests that although there are some problems at present a comfortable midpoint can be reached.

Financially speaking, this rune can indicate that the time is right to buy or sell. It may also show that you are about to receive information or a message of some sort, probably by phone. It could be unexpected news or come at an unexpected time.

Often RAIDHO may indicate that you are of two minds about a problematical situation, feeling that either course could turn out well. If this situation is ambiguous, be on the lookout. If RAIDHO falls with negative runes, it is a strong counsel against placing any faith in the words of others. Pay close attention to the small print in any transactions you may undertake at this time. If paired with PERDHRO reversed, it shows broken promises; with EOLH reversed, it shows that you may be taken for a ride.

Reversed: All the areas which are commonly ascribed to RAIDHO take on a bad tone when reversed. It can indicate a journey which you must undertake even though it may come at an unexpected time or for an unexpected reason. Often it shows a visit to a sick friend or relation, but occasionally it will show other people coming to visit you at a bad time.

This rune reversed can indicate problems in transit, such as delays, breakdowns, or perhaps even an accident. Look to the surrounding runes. You may wish to consider a postponement of your journey, if possible.

Reversed, RAIDHO can indicate an upsetting of your plans. At this time, you will probably come out on the bad end of any commercial transactions or negotiations you may be contemplating, and you should pay close attention to your personal relationships now as well. Ruptures are more likely than reconciliations, and one should try extra hard to be patient and keep up a good sense of humor when dealing with friends or loved ones.

KENAZ

KENAZ symbolizes the element *fire*, but unlike FEHU (whose fiery attributes will be discussed at length in the section on magick), it is the friendly, warm, controlled flame of the torch or the hearth fire.

This rune represents *strengths, energy,* and *power*. Like URUZ, it is a significator of vigorous good health and strong powers of recuperation.

In a runecast, it is often placed to indicate the importance of a good positive attitude. KENAZ is one of the most helpful runes that can arise when you are experiencing problems of any sort. Upright, it is a protective sign, indicating an upcoming respite from worries and a time when trials will be few and easily manageable.

This rune can herald a time of *opening up*, of good things coming into your life. Now would be a good time for you to start something new—perhaps even a new romantic relationship.

In questions of romance, KENAZ will always signify the man in the relationship, no matter what sex the querent may be. It usually shows the male offering something to the female, be it a material gift, such as jewelry or flowers, or a verbal gift, such as a declaration of love. If the querent is male, the surrounding runes indicate whether this gift will be accepted or not. If the querent is female, look to nearby runes for clues to the motives behind this proffered gift.

It is a rune of *creativity* and as such is especially important to artists and craftsmen. It can signify an actual birth when appearing alongside ING, BEORC, or HAGALL. With ANSUZ, RAIDHO, WUNJO or EOLH, it shows the birth of an idea, something creative, sometimes inspired by love.

Reversed: Instead of signifying opening up and new beginnings, KENAZ reversed shows an ending. Rather than a gift, it signifies a loss or an offer that will be withdrawn.

When associated with delay runes like ISA, NIED, or OTHEL reversed, this loss or delay will act to block your progress, generating much internal trauma and anxiety.

You may feel as though you have exercised poor judgment in matters to date or that your vision has been in some way obscured, leading to confusion and a confounding of your problems.

When appearing reversed in a reading pertaining to romance, it can indicate a situation in which the two people involved have done all they were meant to do together and now will go their separate ways. This is especially true when NIED or NIED reversed appears in the runecast. If this is the case, ponder the wisdom of letting go. Do not cling to any relationship which may be failing at this time. Whether the relationship is a business or a personal one, accept the changes that come as perhaps bad but necessary, and prepare your heart for the new growth that is sure to come.

GIFU

The meaning of **GIFU** is *gift*, and this rune is truly a gift to gladden your heart when you see it in your runecast. This is the first rune we have encountered so far that has no reversed position; therefore, it almost always acts in a positive fashion wherever it occurs. If GIFU should occur in the result position, it is a very good sign, signifying a fortuitous outcome to any undertaking made during the time span indicated by the reading.

GIFU usually indicates a *partnership* of some sort, either in business or in love, and it is not uncommon for this rune to herald an important development in a romantic relationship. This could be a commitment of marriage or the cementing of a long-term relationship of some sort. Be careful to examine the runes surrounding GIFU to truly ascertain its meaning as it relates to your situation at the time. Listen to your intuition.

This rune can also indicate a gift or generosity of some sort coming into your life. It could be an emotional gift given in love or a material gift of a timely nature, such as money coming to you in a jam or an item which you have been needing.

Sometimes, however, GIFU will turn up in a runecast only to signify that the problem has roots of an emotional nature.

Often this rune will appear when there is about to be relief from your troubles, and it usually betokens a time of peace and contentment in your life.

WUNJO

Another of the positive runes, **WUNJO** means *joy* and when upright will always represent joy and happiness coming into your life. It is an excellent omen in a runecast, especially in the result position where it indicates the positive outcome of whatever is troubling you at this time. The shift that was due has arrived, the Wheel of Karma has turned in your favor, and you are about to "come to yourself" in some way. Be happy!

In combination with other runes, it indicates *success* in whatever areas they rule. For example, with travel runes such as RAIDHO or EHWAZ, it can show a fortunate and pleasing journey; with message runes such as ANSUZ, it can mean the receipt of good news; when WUNJO falls with love-related runes, it can indicate deep affection and lasting emotional happiness.

Often, WUNJO will signify the object of the inquirer's affections. In this case, it usually shows some activity undertaken with this person ending in a happy result.

It can also represent a joy in one's work, especially if that work is artistic or creative in nature. This rune often appears, like KENAZ, in readings for people who are artists or craftsmen and shows that this creative element is very important to their personal happiness and well-being.

Reversed: The meaning of WUNJO reversed is exactly the opposite of its meaning upright. Things are slow in coming to fruition, and you may be undergoing a difficult or crisis time at present with much attendant misery and unhappiness.

The runes around WUNJO should indicate the problem areas. Paired with RAIDHO or EHWAZ, it can show an unsafe or unsuccessful journey with breakdowns or delays likely.

If the question relates to employment, WUNJO reversed can indicate dissatisfaction, either with the job itself or with your performance in it.

In matters of love, this rune shows a disappointment or a delay of some type in a relationship at present, the intensity of which can be discerned from the surrounding runes.

In all questions relating to business, travel or

love, WUNJO reversed shows a need for caution, perhaps even the putting off of an important decision until a more auspicious time.

This rune can also indicate trouble caused by a third party in the form of frictions and delays. Be especially on the lookout at this time for any possible double-dealing on the part of associates or opponents.

HAGALL

HAGALL means *hail* and with ISA and NIED is a primary rune of *limitations* and *delays*. This rune represents *all forces outside your control.*

It is a symbol of elemental disruption. This disruption may be either good or bad, but due to the fact that the forces bearing upon your life at this time are mostly impersonal ones, it usually takes on a negative tone.

Often HAGALL will turn up when you are thinking of taking a risk of some sort. In this case, the surrounding runes will indicate whether or not this risk will pay off. If paired with FEHU or JERA, it can show eventual success but only with much hard work and effort. If paired with PERDHRO, however, it may show an unexpected gain, such as the lottery or the like. If any of these runes are reversed, the indications are definitely negative, and any risk or gamble should be avoided.

Sometimes this rune will appear to show that your future at this time is in the hands of another. Because HAGALL is such an impersonal rune, usually this "another" is a faceless official or someone with no personal interest in you whatsoever. Often you will learn of this control in a secondhand fashion or through an official letter.

HAGALL is a firm indication that the time is not right for any new starts. In life, sometimes delays and limitations are necessary—learn from them, live with them, and try to be content. Trying to fight against Fate or circumstance at this time will only bring you grief. Now is a time to step back a bit and try to go with the flow.

This rune can sometimes foretell a disruptive natural event, such as an illness, a birth, or perhaps even a death. Often this disruption will be a major but temporary one, lasting only for the duration of the reading.

Indeed, in an otherwise positive runecast, HAGALL can merely signify an interruption rather than a disruption, especially when paired with other delay runes such as ISA, NIED, or OTHEL reversed. This interruption may be the catalyst that causes you to totally change your direction in life, but again, much depends on the surrounding runes, especially the ones immediately following HAGALL in the runecast.

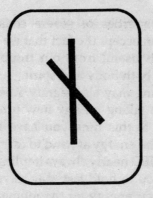

NIED

One of the three great runes of delay, the counsel of **NIED** is one of *patience*. You may find yourself enmeshed in delays, constraints, ill health or oppression, but this rune indicates that tiresome though these may be they will work out in their own good time, and no amount of haste or worry on your part will cause them to work out any faster.

NIED always indicates a time of *passing through a difficult learning situation*. This time is known as "crossing the abyss" by many occult writers and is often a time of extreme emotional travail. However, meeting this emotional challenge head-on and conquering your fear of it can be the catalyst that drives you to overcome whatever obstacles may appear in your path later.

Many philosophies speak of the character

building properties of severe constraint, and when we can accept the fact that we often learn much that is useful from our troubles, we are evolving in both body and spirit.

This rune may also signify a need to *think twice* before taking on any new projects, for it shows that at this time you have neither the ability nor the energy at hand to carry them successfully. NIED nearly always implies *failure*, and it advises you to hold fast, stay as you are, and conserve your energy for the moment.

NIED in association with health runes will often indicate ill health, perhaps even a chronic illness or affliction. When associated with strong, upright health runes like KENAZ, however, it shows an alleviation of illness or perhaps even a cure, especially when the surrounding runes are positive.

In questions of romance, this rune implies that you are ruled by some sort of emotional need which is not being met to your satisfaction at this time.

This rune indicates your *needs* as opposed to your wants, and when it appears, you should ask yourself if you are distressed over minor inconveniences which you may be selfishly blowing out of proportion, or if you truly have a problem.

Reversed: Whenever NIED comes up reversed in a runecast, you should certainly think twice before doing anything you may have planned. This rune reversed often shows you setting off on an improper course of action. If you continue on, NIED warns of inevitable failure and despair.

Make no hasty judgments, and do not act out of impatience, for at this time your actions can only lead to disaster.

If it is too late and you have already become stuck on the wrong path, this rune's message is to be honest and admit to your error, trying to salvage whatever you can from the situation.

Paired with WYRD or JERA, it indicates that now is the time when you will be called upon to make some sort of restitution for past misdeeds. WYRD indicates that it will be a karmic type of retribution, whereas with JERA it is likely to show that the law is about to catch up with you.

If you are not honest with yourself and others at this time and are not willing to accept what is rightly your due, you will find that some force outside your control will step in to see that you do pay. When NIED reversed is paired with HAGALL, that "outside force" could be God; if paired with WYRD, it will be the force of Fate. You could tangle with the justice system or official bureaucracy if JERA is nearby.

ISA

As the name of this rune implies, **ISA** signifies a *cessation of activities*—a freeze. All plans should be put on hold for the moment to be resumed at a more auspicious time.

When associated with other delay runes, it shows that any real positive accomplishments are unlikely now. Delays and frustrations are sure to be a problem, but unless surrounded by very negative runes, they will only be temporary.

ISA often indicates *a cooling trend in a relationship*—whether it is a business or an emotional relationship will be shown by the runes directly following it. There will be ill feelings and resentments, perhaps even a separation or a severance of ties.

In an emotional relationship, the problem is most often a breach of loyalty on the part of another, but sometimes it can indicate disloyalty on the part of the querent. Unless coupled with love runes that are reversed, however, this will usually be resolved within a fairly short time.

When ISA comes up in a runecast that is strongly negative, it could signify that the cooling trend has gone too far to be salvageable. If this is the case, you would do well to move on to a more profitable project or relationship that will bring you more contentment.

JERA

The meaning of this rune is *harvest*, and a *reaping of rewards for efforts expended* is what it signifies. These rewards can be karmic in nature, as in a good deed returned for a good deed done, or they can be a repayment for an outlay of time or money in the past.

JERA is also the rune of *justice* and *legalities* of every kind, and it sometimes appears in a runecast as an indication that the querent is concerned about some legal matter, although it does not always signify a positive outcome.

Because the harvest can only come after an expenditure of energy and care, JERA implies that events must come to fruit in their own good time. Sometimes the delay in question can be a legal issue of some kind, such as the delay involved in financing a home or obtaining a divorce, especially if NIED occupies a prominent position in the runecast.

In the result position, JERA usually shows a positive outcome to the dilemma at hand, often utilizing legal help.

If the runecast is primarily negative, this will not be the case. All is not lost, however, for if JERA is in the result position of a negative runecast, it implies that many of the failures and problems alluded to in the previous runes could be alleviated through a more diligent effort on the part of the individual in question.

Paired with WYRD, NIED, or HAGALL, JERA is often showing a tendency to follow a path for which the querent is not suited. Especially with WYRD, it indicates that by doing so s/he is tempting Fate.

It can also be a warning not to speak ill of others before all the relevant facts are known.

EIHWAZ

To the ancients, the *yew* which this rune symbolizes was a powerful ally in their daily lives. It was the most important tree to the Nordic peoples, more important even than the oak, being not only the best tree for making their formidable longbows but also the tree Yggdrasil, the Great Tree which forms all the nine worlds of men and spirits in Nordic mythology. This rune has powerful associations with *protection*.

EIHWAZ indicates you have set your sights on a reasonable target and are well able to achieve your goals. There may be a slight obstacle in your path, but do not be overeager to move ahead. This may not be a time when you can influence outcomes, and even a delay could prove ultimately beneficial.

No matter how bad things may seem, if

EIHWAZ is sitting in a prominent place in your runecast, it indicates that things will turn around for the better.

It can merely show a slight delay or minor trauma which either will never fully materialize or else will eventually turn out in your favor. Look to the runes following EIHWAZ for a clue as to what will occur.

This rune informs you that only through foresight, perseverance and right action can difficulties be avoided. Look ahead in your life. Are there any upcoming situations which appear doubtful? If so, try to anticipate problems which may arise. Caught in time, most tragedies can be turned into triumphs with the power of EIHWAZ to aid you.

Sometimes EIHWAZ will herald the solving of a matter which has remained hidden for quite some time. This is especially indicated when paired with runes such as ANSUZ or JERA.

PERDHRO

This rune itself is a *mystery* rune, both in a magickal as well as in a literal sense. Experts cannot seem to agree on a meaning for this pictograph. Some have called it a "chessman," others a "dice cup" or a device for casting lots, and one has even suggested it to be the meaning of a "tune," or music.

In divination, however, its meaning is clear. It deals with *things hidden, secrets, and occult abilities.*

PERDHRO in a runecast usually is an indication that something that has remained hidden is about to come to light. This something is usually positive, such as a new opportunity or perhaps a retrieval of an object thought to be lost for good. However, this rune can also refer to the disclosure of a secret, one which you may have been trying very hard to keep to yourself.

This is also a rune of *unexpected gains and surprises* and often shows an unearned gain of money, especially when paired with THURISAZ, GIFU, HAGALL or WYRD. Sometimes this money is in the form of a gift, and since PERDHRO has so many associations with secrecy, examine the surrounding runes closely because the giver's motives could be suspect.

In emotional matters, when this rune falls with URUZ, GIFU, KENAZ, WUNJO, TIR, BEORC or LAGAZ, it indicates extreme sexual compatability on the part of the two persons involved. When the runes URUZ, KENAZ or TIR appear reversed, however, it can show that the relationship is at present based primarily on sexual attraction and that it will surely fail if an effort is not made to relate to one another on other levels.

Falling with negative runes, PERDHRO may foretell an illness of some sort which will be found to be unresponsive to regular medical treatments. If this is the case, try a more unorthodox form of medicine such as acupuncture, acupressure, herbal medicines or magickal healing.

PERDHRO may also indicate a strong intuitive or occult ability on the part of the querent that may soon be called upon to help him or her through a difficult time of life.

Reversed: PERDHRO reversed signifies that events may not turn out as you had hoped. Do not expect too much at this time. You may be overwhelmed by the obstacles in your path at present, but take heart.

This rune means unpleasant surprises and nasty secrets. If you have any skeletons in your closet, PERDHRO reversed suggests that they are about to be uncovered. Be very cautious at this time.

PERDHRO often will herald a disappointment by another person, perhaps even a close friend. Usually this disappointment is financial. Do not invest or loan money, especially to a friend, for the duration of this runecast. You may find it very difficult to recover, and if you do get it back at all, it may only be with much grief.

In an emotional sense, this rune reversed indicates sexual problems of some sort, and if the runes TIR, URUZ or KENAZ are reversed as well or if ISA is present, it shows that one partner no longer finds the other attractive. Whether this will work itself out or not can be discerned from the surrounding runes and the general tone of the runecast.

On certain occasions, this rune can also indicate a period of unwise experimentation with occult forces, getting much more than you had expected. Always make certain you are familiar with your occult operations, and more importantly, understand your reasons for performing them and the symbolism they contain.

EOLH

EOLH signifies a *fortunate new influence* entering your life, often through unconscious emotions or *instincts*.

This influence could be a new career opportunity or course of study. EOLH is a rune of *friendship* and often shows a new relationship with someone who is outgoing, generous and fun to be around.

EOLH is a very strong *protective* rune, and its appearance usually indicates that you will be protected from any misfortune for the period of time covered by the reading.

Often, if harm does threaten, you will receive a very strong premonition of disaster that enables you to avoid whatever problems may arise. Look to the other runes in the reading, and use your intuition at this time.

This is a very beneficial rune.

Reversed: EOLH reversed is a sign of vulnerability, of sacrifice with no personal gain. Usually this rune reversed indicates that you are being deceived and misled by others; all of the forces you are expending are for their benefit and not your own. Often, you will be made the scapegoat for other people's failures.

This rune can show an offer which should be refused or a person to be avoided. Watch all of the associations you form at this time. If you must become involved with dubious individuals who will use you, be aware of the fact and try to turn the situation around to your own advantage. In this way you will eventually benefit.

On occasion, you may find that you are deceived not by others but by yourself. You may be expecting something for nothing, and your greed and naiveté make you ripe for being conned at this time, especially in business or financial matters.

In questions of love, EOLH counsels delay in new relationships until more is known about your partner's character and motives.

SIGEL

SIGEL, along with TIR, is one of the great runes of *victory*, and its appearance in the runecast virtually assures success. It is a rune of *great power*, and much power will be available to you at this time to effect changes in your life. Any opposition you may encounter can be swiftly overcome, leaving you time to relax and take it easy.

Sometimes SIGEL's appearance suggests that worry and tension have begun to take their toll. When surrounded by business runes, such as RAIDHO and WUNJO, or material runes, like OTHEL or FEHU, it could show that you are being a workaholic and sorely in need of a little rest and relaxation.

In this case, if the associated runes are negative, it could indicate that you often worry a great deal about your problems but can never seem to get up enough motivation to do anything about them.

Often this rune refers to the sort of person who is very self-centered and who wants to be totally in charge of his or her life at all times. If this cannot be done, anxiousness and helplessness set in. Runes to be on the lookout for in this case are WYRD, HAGALL, ISA, NIED and THURISAZ, especially NIED.

SIGEL is a rune of *great health and vitality*, and sometimes it turns up in the runecast to indicate that the person in question is concerned about his or her health. Positive runes to look for are those which denote a strong and positive life force, such as KENAZ and TIR, or the runes GIFU, DAEG and ING, which show strong powers of recovery.

This rune has no reversed position and is nearly always positive.

TIR

TIR is the other great rune of victory, representing *success in any competition*. The competitive spirit is embodied in this rune as in no other, and this spirit will probably permeate your life for the duration of the reading. This rune can indicate that you are about to take up a "cause," or have already done so. It usually concerns the "forces of fair play" versus the "forces of unjust oppression." You are ready to fight for what you believe in, no matter what the odds, and, depending on the other runes, of course, you will probably succeed.

This is a rune of *extreme motivation*, showing a strength of will and a singleness of mind that can enable you to overcome all odds. Look to the surrounding runes, however. When TIR is coupled with other success-related runes, such as FEHU,

75

URUZ and SIGEL, it shows that you will keep up the fight and go from strength to strength tearing up the opposition, but when associated with negative or delay runes, it shows that no matter how strong your determination may be, this time the opposition will prevail.

TIR often shows an *increase in money or power*, sometimes both. This rune shows you rising up in the world through your own abilities and strength of character.

This rune is an excellent omen in all questions of love and relationships. It can indicate a timely new romance, filled with happiness and passion.

TIR is mainly a *masculine* rune, and in the runecast it represents the male querent; if the querent is female, TIR indicates the most important man in her life, the one she is interested in the most. This will usually be the newest man to enter her life—the new flame over the old, the lover rather than the husband, etc.

If TIR is upright, this man's intentions are good, but if it is reversed, he may not be being totally honest with you, and you will have cause to challenge his motives. PERDHRO reversed paired with TIR tells you that the relationship is based on sexual attraction alone. If TIR upright is paired with WUNJO, it signifies an affectionate and lasting relationship.

If the querent is male, TIR is usually indicative of his strength of will. If the querent is female, this rune can also indicate a man who will come to her aid in the troubles at hand. He will always be someone she respects or looks up to in some way.

In a woman's runecast, when TIR is paired with LAGAZ, it shows that it is she who will take the active part and act on her own behalf in regard to her problems.

In a man's reading coupled with MANNAZ, it often signifies help from superiors or powerful friends.

This rune can also indicate a *quick recovery from illness*.

Reversed: TIR reversed stands for waning enthusiasm, failure in competitive enterprises and a lack of fidelity in both love and friendship.

This rune often signifies an impeded energy flow on some level. It can indicate a dearth of ideas and creative thoughts and often shows extreme impatience on the part of the querent. When paired with delay runes in an otherwise positive reading, it could indicate that you are experiencing the "dark before the dawn," and if you can remain patient, things will certainly improve.

For a male, it can show that you are inclined to give up in the face of difficulties and are unlikely to make much of an effort on your behalf. It indicates that you expect good things to drop into your lap by divine right, and if they don't, you give up. When paired with LAGAZ in a woman's reading, the meaning is much the same.

In love matters, TIR reversed shows that any relationship now going on will not reach a permanent conclusion. Sometimes it may indicate dwindling passion on the male's behalf. It shows misunderstandings and difficulties in communication; whether this will lead to a reconciliation or an eventual separation can be discerned from the surrounding runes. Be careful at this time of "wearing your heart on your sleeve"— you may get hurt.

BEORC

This is a fertility rune—a rune of *birth* and of the *family*. In a runecast, **BEORC** often represents your mother or your children, and it usually indicates an event which brings joy to the family, such as a birth or a wedding. Beorc represents your *true home*, the "home where your heart is" as opposed to where you may be living now.

BEORC always presages a birth, whether it is an actual birth or the formation of an idea.

Go into matters at this time with care and awareness. This rune is always indicative of a tangible result and is a very helpful rune whenever a new project is being contemplated. It suggests that any schemes in the works should be implemented right away.

In the result position, BEORC indicates a fortunate outcome to any question asked; in other positions, it can often signify a new beginning—a new project, a new romance—which will bring much happiness. When BEORC is surrounded by positive runes, it shows a favorable outcome, while negative runes indicate that your success will be short-lived.

For people who wish to have children but have had no luck, this rune signifies eventual success, especially when paired with ING.

Reversed: BEORC reversed will usually indicate family problems and domestic troubles. It shows much friction between you and those closest to you.

BEORC reversed is not a portent of certain doom; it is merely a warning, unless surrounded by truly negative runes. On its own, it does not point to a permanent split or irreconcilable differences.

This rune reversed can forecast an unfortunate family situation or foretell the receipt of worrisome news about a family member. Frequently, its presence signifies anxiety about someone close to you. Surrounding runes should be examined for clues as to who this someone is, such as GIFU for your spouse or partner, ANSUZ for a child, or OTHEL for an older relative.

When the question relates solely to business, it usually indicates that any venture contemplated now will fall through, but as it is not a totally negative rune even when reversed, it may merely be showing that through prudence, restraint, and timely action these plans could be brought to fruit at a later time.

EHWAZ

EHWAZ is a rune of *physical movement, physical shifts, or new dwelling places*. Its main significance is change, but a change for the better and usually an anticipated one. This change will usually involve travel of some sort, perhaps even an actual change of locale. EHWAZ stands for *gradual development and steady progress*.

It can mean a journey by land, especially when paired with RAIDHO, ANSUZ or BEORC. ANSUZ reversed suggests a sick relative; RAIDHO, a journey for pleasure; and BEORC, a family get-together.

EHWAZ in a prominent place suggests that whatever your question, you are tackling the problem in the correct spirit and are close to success. Sometimes with a rune of outside help, such as ANSUZ, JERA or MANNAZ, it can show a person whose good judgment and common sense will aid you in whatever is troubling you at this time.

Reversed: EHWAZ is the one rune that does not automatically assume a negative meaning when reversed. If grouped with positive runes, it can mean exactly the same reversed as it does upright.

Sometimes it will indicate a far journey, especially if paired with LAGAZ. If paired with RAIDHO, the journey will only be a temporary one, but it will be one for pleasure.

In some cases, especially when coupled with a rune such as URUZ, it may show a sudden or unexpected change. Unless associated with negative runes, it is not likely to be a bad change.

However, when EHWAZ reversed is with other negative runes, its counsel is to hold fast and not implement any changes you may be considering at this time as they are likely to result in misfortune and loss. Be sure that what you are or are not doing is timely.

MANNAZ

MANNAZ is the rune of *humankind*. It is a rune of *interdependence*, and you can expect to receive some sort of aid or cooperation regarding the problem at hand. This aid could very well come in the form of good advice, and as with ANSUZ, this advice will be totally honest and unbiased.

Sometimes this rune appears in reference to the individual in the reading. In this case, it can indicate that you may be becoming too caught up in the problem to be effective in solving it. In conjunction with negative runes, it shows that you have blown it all out of proportion and are about to give up altogether.

This is the time to seek out that good advice mentioned earlier and to try to adopt a more positive, progressive attitude.

When associated with positive runes, MANNAZ can indicate that now is a good time to implement any new plans; however, if surrounded by delay runes such as NIED, ISA, or OTHEL and ANSUZ reversed, it suggests that the time is not right at present for any fresh projects.

This rune may signal a time when you need to take special care to remain modest. Now may not be the time to take credit for any accomplishments. Examine your situations at present, look to the runes, and be aware.

MANNAZ can indicate magickal ability, especially if paired with PERDHRO or LAGAZ.

However, MANNAZ with LAGAZ can also indicate that the querent is having problems at this time with women in general, no matter what the querent's sex.

Reversed: This rune indicates that you can expect no help in your predicament from any fellow human for the duration of your reading.

Chances are good that you will run into all kinds of subversions and obstructions of your plans at this time. Sometimes your adversary is an individual, but more often it is a group of people who see fit to interfere in your business. In this case, the runes around MANNAZ will show you how to deal with them. Paired with ISA or NIED, it suggests waiting before acting; with JERA, it indicates legal means. TIR counsels "fighting fire with fire."

The message of MANNAZ can also be that

at this time you are your own worst enemy. When relating to the individual, it is a prime indicator of selfishness and can show that your self-centeredness is the root of your problem. Try seeing things from someone else's point of view for a change.

It can also indicate a way of life alien to you, perhaps a foreign country or a foreign person. Often this person will hold a sexual interest for you. In an otherwise positive runecast, this can be the meaning of MANNAZ.

LAGAZ

LAGAZ is a rune of *intuitive knowledge* and indicates you should follow your intuitions closely in the matter in question.

Sometimes, especially with PERDHRO, it can indicate definite psychic abilities, or it can show that you are being guided and protected now by higher powers. Usually you will never be consciously aware of this guidance.

For those not naturally psychic, it can show a significant event or a prophetic dream regarding a potentially hazardous situation or a bad offer. Success at this time lies in tuning in to your inner voice.

LAGAZ is the principal *female* rune and will usually symbolize the querent in the runecast if the querent is female. For a female, LAGAZ indicates that no matter what troubles beset her she will be more than capable of dealing with them.

In a man's reading, it shows the presence of a strong and supportive female in the background, possibly the most important woman in his life.

This rune speaks of a *good memory* and *success in learning,* usually through utilization of imaginative faculties.

It frequently shows that the tide has turned in your favor and can indicate that a time of relaxing, re-evaluating and cleansing is at hand.

LAGAZ in a result position signifies that you will meet with a sympathetic and understanding response from others who can be called upon to help you solve your problem.

Reversed: Unless backed with very positive runes, LAGAZ reversed is a very bad sign indeed. It shows that you will be or already are misled by your intuition into tackling something for which you have no real aptitude. This rune is a temptation to do the wrong thing or to take the easy way out, which can only lead to trouble.

Unless coupled with delay runes, this rune speaks against a "wait and see" attitude. You should take action immediately to get out of any bad situation.

LAGAZ reversed can indicate a woman who may bring trouble into your life. It can mean betrayal and backstabbing on the part of a female friend, or for a male, it can also indicate disloyalty on the part of an existing partner or a new love affair that will only bring unhappiness.

If surrounded by success runes, it can indicate a strong female figure who may be a great help at present but who will make you feel beholden later.

This rune can often indicate a failure to call upon the wisdom of your instincts, especially when paired with PERDHRO.

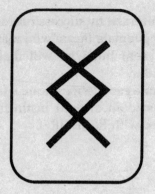

ING

ING is almost always a positive rune, and only in the most negative of runecasts does it even suggest failure. It indicates that the force is available to you at this time to complete any projects, and it shows a *successful conclusion* to the problem at hand.

It also represents the sense of *relief* that comes from a positive accomplishment, but it can also merely indicate a mind free from anxiety.

ING is a very important rune and could signal an event which will prove to be a milestone in your life such as the birth of a child (especially with BEORC), a new job (as with FEHU) or a new love affair (with GIFU or WUNJO).

This rune indicates the ending of an old phase of life to give birth to a new and more exciting one. This rune marks a time of positive energies and deliverance, and when it turns up in your runecast, you may be assured of good fortune.

DAEG

DAEG is symbolic of *increase and growth*, and a major period of increase and prosperity is often introduced by this rune. It has no negative aspects, and even in a negative reading it shows that you possess the inner strength to turn your situation around if only you will utilize it.

When it is paired with delay runes, it alleviates their negativity, pointing to an eventual victory over obstacles.

The growth symbolized by this rune is slow but steady, rather than overnight success. Therefore, as the changes are happening, you may not notice them, but one day you will wake up and things will look much brighter.

DAEG has much to do with your attitude. It suggests, as with KENAZ, that putting up a good face will do much to help you in your present problem. If DAEG is associated with WUNJO reversed, MANNAZ reversed, OTHEL reversed or HAGALL, it indicates that through your constant dwelling upon problems or obstacles you are drawing those very things to you.

Sometimes, drawing this rune will mark a major change in your life, perhaps something so radical that you will never live your life in the same way again. Usually this deals with making a new start on some level, but sometimes it shows that you must make the best of a situation over which you have no control. Things will get better though, perhaps through an outside agency. This is especially indicated when MANNAZ is nearby.

It can also show you being exposed to a new way of life or of thinking—even a religious enlightenment.

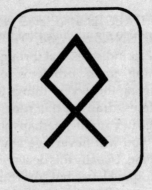

OTHEL

OTHEL is a rune of *possessions* and usually represents the things that money can buy, usually land or a building. When it does indicate money, it will be money in the form of inheritances, trusts or pension funds.

Surrounded by runes like FEHU, BEORC, NIED or WUNJO, it shows a materialist or a tightwad. Sometimes though, especially when paired with SIGEL, it signifies a hard worker, someone who expects to work long and hard to fulfill wants and who is totally comfortable with that idea.

Often, it indicates one who is consumed by an *ideal* or *vision*, perhaps one inspired by the past. Runes to look for in this context are ANSUZ and MANNAZ.

Upright, it also suggests help in the matter at

hand from older people or perhaps old friends.
   It can also signify *inherited traits*.

Reversed: Delay and frustration. In a prominent
position, OTHEL could indicate difficulties encountered through trying to progress too fast.
Continuing on in haste could permanently
damage the outcome of the relationship or problem at hand.

   When coupled with positive runes, OTHEL
reversed merely signifies that success is still
possible although it may be further off than you'd
like at the time. In this case, be patient. It can also
show that eventual success hinges on thorough-
ness and attention to detail.

   Reversed, it is indicative of the individual
standing on his or her own two feet. It can show
that you have a "poor little rich kid" attitude
toward life, but in this case you are faced with
something that you can't buy your way out of. In
fact, OTHEL reversed signifies that you can
expect no financial help, either from family or
from organizations.

   Often this rune will show that even legal
methods won't help, for while OTHEL is reversed,
trying to "buck the system" or turn it to your own
advantage is a fruitless proposition.

PRINCIPLES OF DIVINATION AND RUNE LAYOUTS

The first thing you must remember is that you are consulting an oracle. You are not "having your fortune told." The oracle is not an absolute, and unlike conventional fortunetelling, it gives you the information and allows you to decide what to make of it. The answers to be found in the runes are the ones to be found in yourself. Seek them, and listen with your inner ear.

The great psychologist and philosopher Carl Jung, quoted in *Rune Games*, was not only familiar with the oracular system but also used it in the form of the I Ching. In his introduction to the I Ching, he had the courage to write: "Theoretical considerations of cause and effect often look pale and dusty in comparison to the practical results of chance."

Consulting the runes places you firmly in the present time, and whatever happens in that given moment possesses what Jung calls "the quality peculiar to that moment." Given your location in the universe at the time, an oracle guides you through the variables and allows you to draw your own conclusions on the matter in question.

When you pose your question, be sure to phrase it in such a way that there is no doubt as to its meaning. In other words, *be specific*. For instance, instead of saying "Should I accept this job and move to North Dakota?" (which is really two questions), perhaps you should say "The issue is my new job." By formulating your query in this fashion, you allow yourself to make a broader interpretation and concentrate on the one main issue, your new job.

If you are casting the runes for another, do not ask what his or her question concerns. If the querent has really thought on the matter and you have familiarized yourself with the basic rune meanings, it should be very easy to discern the subject of the question, be it love, finance, health or business. By not being told the question, you eliminate any conscious bias you may have in the matter and that dangerous tendency to play "Dear Abby," giving your own advice rather than that indicated by the runes.

There are a number of different runic layouts to be found in the works of various authors. A few of them are very good and will also be illustrated here. However, in my opinion, some have been invented that are much more complex than is really necessary, especially for the novice. The other thing that I dislike about them is that they are all too often based on Tarot spreads, which aren't runic. I feel that the runes are a simple, earthy system and its layouts should also retain a bit of simplicity.

You should have no trouble using the layouts contained herein to find out the answers to even complex problems, but in case you do or just want more examples of runic layouts, there are several good sources to be found in the suggested reading list, notably *The Runic Workbook* and *Rune Games*.

In ancient times, runes were cast in a very simple, straightforward process. We have record of it in the writings of Tacitus in chapter 10 of *Germania:*

"They take the wood from the branch of a fruit-bearing tree and cut it into slips, marking each with a distinctive sign. They then scatter the lots at random on a piece of white cloth. An official priest (if it is a matter of great importance) or the head of the household (if it is a private matter) prays to the gods, and looking up to the sky, picks up each slip one at a time and interprets them in accordance with the signs etched upon them."

This excerpt from the histories of a contemporary of the Teutonic runemasters is, as far as can be determined, factual and tells us two important things.

First, it tells us that the runes were chosen at

random as they are in all of the methods in use today. This random choice, especially when accompanied by prayer and earnest concentration, ensured that each rune selected was placed in the hands of the diviner directly by an outside force. In the mind of the magician, the Norns and Odin and Freya acted directly through the runes to guide the people. This is why it is traditional even today to ask them for guidance before any rune-cast. By trying to get in touch with these Energies, we can draw closer to an understanding of how they acted on the lives of the rune users, and through this understanding we can glean more information on the runes themselves.

The second thing that this passage tells us is that it is not only an elite "magician class" who used the runes, but that anyone could use them, although this right usually went by virtue of seniority to the head of the household. This indicates that the runes were very familiar to ordinary people, who used them frequently for various purposes.

Earlier in this book, I spoke of the importance of ritual, and doubtless I shall mention it again. Ritual is one of the best ways to prime your subconscious to receive the information that the runes will give you. Through ritual, all mundane and trivial thoughts are exorcised, leaving the mind blank as a slate, ready to receive the impressions of the runes. This stillness of mind is very important to an accurate runecast.

Following is a sample ritual based on the

method recorded by Tacitus. Whether you choose to use this method, devise your own, or dispense with the ritual altogether is entirely up to you. It is more important when doing any magickal operation to feel comfortable with what you are doing over all other considerations. Always listen to your inner voice.

Sample Ritual

First, lay out your rune cloth on the spot where you intend to perform your divination. See that its corners point to the Four Directions, if they can be ascertained. Stand near the southern edge, hold the runes in your hand, and concentrate on your question. Let the runes tumble out of your pouch onto the cloth, saying "Urdhr, Verthandi, Skuld!" (the Three Norns) as they hit the ground. Turn all of the ones with symbols showing face downwards on the cloth.

Using your right hand, shuffle and swirl the runes around in a clockwise motion until you feel they are mixed up enough. Then, hold your hands palm downwards about three or four inches above the runes and quiet your mind in preparation for the choices you are about to make. Many rune magicians will use this pause to once again call upon Odin and Freya to request a truthful and revealing runecast.

A simple prayer, should you choose to use one, might be something like this:

O mighty Odin, Master of the Runes,
And lovely Freya, Goddess of the Best and Good,
Please guide my hands and my thoughts
That I may receive a true reading.
For at this time I am in great need
Of information and comfort.
Guide me by your hand
And by the powers of Wind, Fire, Earth, and Water.
So mote it be!

With your palms still held over the runes, shut your eyes and concentrate on your palms. Can you feel the energy interaction between your palms and the runes? You should. It will feel like a tingling sensation or a cool, continuous breath of air. This shows that you are properly attuned for the reading and assures a truer interaction between you and your runes.

With your eyes still closed, use your right hand and slowly pass it over the rune pieces. Note any piece which seems more "energetic" than the others, and pick it up. Place each rune (still face down) in its corresponding location in the runic layout. For example, when you choose your first rune, place it in the space marked 1 in your layout diagram, and so forth. Do not turn the rune. Whether the rune is upright or reversed is very important, so it should not be turned around in the hand after it has been chosen for the runecast.

Once all the required runes have been chosen, it is time to turn them face up. Whether your runes are round or rectangular, the method is the same. Turn over each rune as if it were a page in a book. This ensures that the symbol as it comes up is facing the same way that it was when it was still lying on the cloth. The rune will either be upright or it will be reversed, and the meaning will vary a great deal depending on the way it is facing. Some runes have no reversed meaning, looking the same either right side up or upside down.

People have different ideas on the number of runes that should be turned over at one time. For the novice, I would suggest only turning over one or two runes at the most and interpreting those before turning over any more, unless the rune layout indicates otherwise. This will enable you to concentrate better on the meaning of each rune as it pertains to the meaning of the space in the layout in which it rests.

Once all of the runes have been turned over, it is a good idea to give the runecast a final once-over. Go through the whole reading in your mind, and pay special attention to any hidden relationships between different runes which may pop up. These "hidden relationships" were discussed a bit in the preceding section, and learning how to recognize rune "partnerships" is often the most important factor in the final outcome of the divination.

For this reason, it is very important to have a thorough knowledge of each rune and the way it relates to its neighbors before seriously attempting divination. These runic forces will be felt differently by each individual as a variety of sensations acting upon your subconscious. Each student should explore the "feel" of each rune on its own terms. Once you have tuned in to the rune force, the feeling will be unmistakable.

The One-Rune Method

The easiest and fastest way to obtain a quick peek at what is acting on your life at present is the One-Rune Method. This is a very good method to use when you have your runes with you but no time or place to effectively perform a longer rune-cast. It consists of simply quieting your mind, concentrating on your question, and drawing out one rune which can be used to ascertain several different things.

This method is used when you know you need some guidance and information about an unknown situation. Simply ask the runes "What do I need to know in my life at this time?" The reply you get will often be comforting as well as enlightening.

It is also good to pull out a rune first thing in the morning to get an idea of what your day will be like. Reach in and ask something like "What will today be like?" or "What do I need to know in order to make the right choices today?" Sometimes it is often useful to repeat this process at night to see how you did.

I use this "morning rune" quite often, and it has helped me on many an occasion to anticipate situations that otherwise would have taken me completely by surprise. No one likes to pull out a reversed or a delay rune first thing on a Monday morning, but if you are aware that today is going to be a really tough day, it allows you to steel yourself for it, and it definitely counsels keeping a sense of humor. There have been many a bad day which I was able to turn around for the better simply by being aware that problems were going to come up and by acting in the proper fashion when they did.

Another way of interpreting this rune is to use it to obtain an insight into the nature of your troubles. If you are experiencing a blockage in your life or cannot seem to figure out what your problems are all about, this rune will show the root of the matter. If the rune is GIFU, for example, the matter is love; with JERA, it could be legalities or red tape; if RAIDHO or EHWAZ, it could be travel, etc. The knowledge of the underlying causes of your problem can often go a long way towards helping you find an answer to it. That is the purpose of this interpretation.

The other way that you might choose to use this rune is to find out the status of a person or even an animal that may have strayed from home. Concentrate on your friend, for example, reach into the pouch and draw out a rune. This will give you an instant status report on his or her condition. This is especially comforting when your friends are traveling and there is no way to contact them via the usual channels or when a relative far away from you is ill.

The Three-Rune Method

This is one of the most widely used runic layouts. It's been given several different names, but here we will just call it the Three-Rune Method. It is not a long-term forecast, but it is useful for gaining insight into what is happening at the moment and how you might deal with it. A very simple but effective method, it can be interpreted in two ways.

First, relax your mind and perform your opening ritual. When all of your thoughts have been stilled and you have the question firmly in

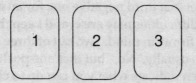

your mind, select three runes at random and place them in front of you on your rune cloth in the order indicated in the illustration, from left to right.

The first and fastest interpretation is for "yes" or "no" questions. A lot of questions fit into this category, such as "Should I quit my job?," or "Should I marry my lover?," and so forth.

If this is the interpretation you choose, turn over all three runes at once. If all three are positive, the answer is an unequivocal "Yes." If all three are reversed or delay runes, then the answer is "No, not now."

More often than not, however, you will have a mixture of positive and negative runes. Since there are an odd number of runes in this runecast, there will still be a predominance of one type or the other. From these you can interpret whether the outcome will be good or bad. Two out of three runes positive often means "Yes," but be sure to interpret that third negative one for an idea as to where difficulties may arise, and keep that information firmly in mind. Two out of three negative runes is usually "No," but that one positive rune will often indicate what you can do to change or temper the negativity of the other two.

Many people want information that is a little more specific than that, and for this we can look to the second method of interpreting this layout.

In this method, one rune at a time is turned over and individually interpreted before going on to the other runes.

The first rune on the far left indicates the *problem* at hand. OTHEL reversed or FEHU reversed here could show that the problem is monetary or is directly brought about due to lack of funds; GIFU or TIR reversed could indicate relationship troubles; URUZ reversed, an illness. This rune often tells you what you already know if the reading is for yourself and is a comforting sign that your runecast is on the right track. If the reading is for another, this rune will tell you what the querent's question is and will aid you in the interpretation of the other two runes.

The center rune suggests what *course* you should take regarding your difficulties. For example, let's say that your first rune was TIR reversed, indicating relationship problems. Your next rune will tell you what to do. If the rune is RAIDHO reversed, you are advised to be extra patient with your partner now because this is likely to be a stressful time for you both. If it is KENAZ, it shows that keeping a good positive attitude will go a long way towards helping you to deal with the problems. Look at this middle rune carefully, check its interpretation and what it may be saying to you, and try to relate it to your first rune.

Your final rune will tell you *what is likely to come about* IF YOU FOLLOW THE ADVICE OF THE SECOND RUNE. Suppose you had OTHEL reversed in the first position, your second rune was FEHU upright and the final rune was ING, which indicates a fortunate outcome. The way these three runes would be read is this: OTHEL reversed tells me that you are out of money and are very worried about your financial status at present. FEHU signifies gain through hard work. If you follow FEHU's advice and work extra hard to accumulate or save money, then you will get to ING, your fortunate outcome.

However, if you continue to merely mope about and do not take the advice of FEHU, then no matter how long you may wait, you will not have a fortunate outcome. In this case, you could not accuse the runes of playing you false. Through your own inaction you have evaded your good fortune, and you have no one to blame but yourself.

This example is yet another affirmation that the runecast is an oracle to help you help yourself, rather than an absolute indicator of unchangeable future events.

The Five-Rune Method

Once again, perform your opening ritual. Select five runes one at a time and lay them face down on your rune cloth in the order shown on the next page. The first three runes represent your *past, present,* and *future,* and it is usually best in this runecast to turn over the center rune first, the one that occupies Position 2. This is the rune of the *present* and will show your problem as it is now. It can also show your state of mind. A negative rune in this position that does not seem to be in synch with the question can often show that you (or your querent) are of a very troubled and agitated state of mind.

The rune in Position 1 signifies the *past* and will tell you what it was in the past that caused you to be in your current position.

Next, read the rune in Position 4. This indicates the *help* that you can expect to receive in the problem at hand. This help will come in the form of tangible aid from other people, your inner reserve of strength, or perhaps (in the case of WYRD or PERDHRO) the Cosmic Forces. If there is a negative rune here, it can indicate an unwillingness to accept the advice given by the runes or another person, or it can indicate delays or slight problems that may impede the speedy

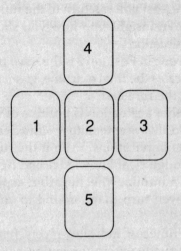

resolution of the matter in question.

Position 5 indicates what *aspects of the problem must be accepted* and cannot be changed. Positive runes here show a lack of troublesome influences and oppositions, while negative runes show the obstacles to your success. When the rune in this position is WYRD, it is telling you that the event foretold is destined to be. This is one of those times when there truly is nothing you can do about the situation—it must find its own end. In this case, look to the runes in Positions 4 and 3. If either or both of these are positive, then WYRD ensures your eventual happiness or success. If the rune in Position 3 is negative, then WYRD indicates certain failure. If the runecast looks bad, at the very least you can turn to the rune in Position 4 for an insight into how you should deal with the situation.

The rune in Position 3 is the *result* rune. This rune indicates the final outcome, given the other factors in the runecast.

Whether a situation is positive or negative, you should always enter into it with a clear knowledge of its implications. Even if the runes look bleak, through clear knowledge and right action you can minimize the negative aspects and perhaps even turn them around to your eventual favor.

This runecast indicates recent future happenings, usually within three months.

The Seven-Rune Method

This runecast gives a bit more detail with more information on how to deal with your problem and on what led you into your present dilemma in the first place. It usually speaks of events three months into the future and into the past.

If you wish to use this layout but want information on happenings more current than three months, be certain to concentrate on your time frame as well when you are concentrating on your question.

The questions you can answer with this layout can be much broader in scope than the questions in the preceding runecasts. Now, instead of asking "yes" or "no" or "What about my

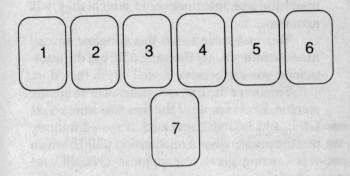

relationship?," you can ask questions like "How will my job progress if I take this new business course?" or "If I started seeing other people, how would my current lover accept it?" Through questions like these, you can certainly get enough information to solve all but the most complex of problems.

Perform your opening ritual and choose seven runes. Lay them out one at a time on your rune cloth in the order shown in the illustration.

In this reading, you will have to be interpreting two runes at a time. This is not simple but is easily grasped once you have a thorough knowledge of the individual runes. Even the two most dissimilar runes can relate to one another, and often the more different the runes are, the more insightful the information is which they will give you.

You may have to do this runecast several times before you get the hang of it, but the information you can receive is well worth the effort.

Turn over the first two runes. These are the *problem*. For example, if the first two runes were GIFU and WUNJO reversed, it would indicate that the problem was a relationship (GIFU) which was causing great unhappiness (WUNJO reversed).

The runes in Positions 3 and 4 are read next. These show the *factors in the past* which have led up to the situation at present. Sometimes these are positive, sometimes not, but they help you to understand the underlying causes of your problem. Through this, you can gain much information that is useful in its resolution.

Positions 5 and 6 are the two most important runes in this runecast. They represent the *advice* the runes are giving you, and extra special care must be taken to interpret their meanings as they relate to one another. They can indicate a need to wait and not act or a need to act immediately. They also may indicate a total shift of emphasis to new realms totally unrelated to the problem in question. In other words, "Don't dwell on this problem, do this instead."

The final position, of course, is the *result* position. Keep in mind that a positive rune in this place (or a negative one, for that matter) will only be truly positive (or negative) if the preceding runes indicate such an outcome.

This is a challenging runecast and certainly worth the time it takes to master it.

THE RUNES IN MAGICK

ᚠ FEHU symbolizes primal, uncontrolled Fire. Its energy is that of the "Big Bang" and of lightning strikes in the wilderness. It is the power of generation at its most basic level. Its energies are totally wild and very useful for magick involving swift, radical changes.

USES: 1. To hasten affairs to their next stage— use after the "subject" runes in your runescript.

2. Increase in monetary wealth.

3. Protection of valuables.

4. The "sending" rune—use it to send either your energy or the energy of the runes out into the formative spheres.

ᚾ This is the rune of changes. URUZ is the shaping power that brings about manifestation. Use it to give sluggish circumstances a little prod. A rune of vitality and strength, it is also useful in any healing magick, especially when the patient is weak and could use some extra strength.

USES: 1. To draw new situations into your life.

2. To initiate new circumstances purely by a force of will.

3. Healing and maintenance of good physical health.

ᚦ THURISAZ is the directed cosmic power of defense. It symbolizes Mjollnir, the Hammer of Thor. It is pure will untempered by self-consciousness. It is a projectable form of applied power. This rune is especially useful in conjunction with ᚠ, ᚲ, ᛋ, ᚾ, ᚦ, and ᛒ —the force of THURISAZ is able to direct their energies in an effective fashion. Use it when a "little something extra" is required to get things off the ground.

USES: 1. New beginnings.

2. Use when you need luck or when circumstances are beyond your control.

3. Protection or defense.

4. Neutralization of enemies or opposition.

5. To push the issue in love magick.

ᚠ ANSUZ is the rune of communications. It rules over song, poetry, examinations, interviews and magickal incantations. It is good to use wherever communication is the issue.

USES: 1. Convincing and magnetic speech.

2. To gain wisdom.

3. Confidence and luck with exams.

4. Increase of active magickal energies.

ᚱ RAIDHO is not only a rune of travel but also rules over the cosmic laws of Right and Order. Therefore, like JERA, it is useful for legal matters, especially when you have been unjustly accused and need to bring those forces of Right to bear on the issue.

USES: 1. Obtaining justice according to Right.

2. Safe and comfortable travel.

〈   KENAZ is another rune of Fire, but unlike FEHU, it is a gentle, more controlled form of Fire which gives the ability and the will to create. It is the rune of the artist and craftsman and is useful either when creativity is the issue or when artistic things are very important to the person for whom you are creating the runescript. It also governs the technical aspects of magick. It is the rune that governs passion, lust, and sexual love as fiery, positive attributes.

USES: 1. Use to strengthen any runescript.

2. Healing, physical well-being.

3. Love, stability and passion in relationships.

4. Fresh starts.

5. Protection of valuables.

✕   GIFU is the rune of partnerships in all realms. It contains the power to integrate the energies of two or more people in order to produce a force that is greater than the sum total of their individual parts. It is the primary rune of sex magick.

USES: 1. Love and sex magick.

2. Increase in magickal powers.

3. Anything to do with partnerships.

4. Mental and physical equilibrium.

ᛈ WUNJO is the rune of "happily ever after." It is generally used in the final position as a significator of success and happiness.

USES: 1. Fulfillment in any area, especially love or career.

2. Success in travel.

ᚺ The meaning of HAGALL in magick is very different from its meanings in divination. In divination, HAGALL indicates frustrating delays but not stagnation. In magick, this rune is a rune of evolution, but it is evolution of the slow but sure type within a fixed framework. Its fixed nature promotes security and keeps negative energies from entering your space.

USES: 1. Protection.

2. Use where luck is needed.

3. To encourage a positive result within a fixed framework.

ᚾ This rune has two aspects to it, and you would do well to remember them when formulating your runescript. NIED represents need and distress but also the release from that distress. Through the utilization of this rune by the will, one can change Fate via knowledge and wisdom. This rune is a very powerful rune in Icelandic love magick and represents the primal needs and desires that drive you to seek out a lover.

USES: 1. Overcoming distress.

2. Achieving your goals.

3. Protection.

4. Love magick—to find a lover.

5. Impetus to get a relationship off the ground.

This rune of ISA rules the forces of inertia and entropy. It is also a symbol of the ego.

USES: 1. To "freeze" a situation as it is.

2. Development of will.

3. Halting of unwanted forces.

JERA is the rune of the harvest, of rewards arriving at their proper time. It also governs legalities of all sorts and is useful in all legal matters.

USES: 1. Use when a tangible result is expected for an outlay of money, time or effort.

2. Helps to bring events to pass.

3. Helps in legal matters.

4. Fertility.

This rune of EIHWAZ, symbolizing the yew tree, is a very powerful rune of banishing and protection.

USES: 1. Protection.

2. Increase in power.

3. Removal of obstacles.

PERDHRO is a rune of time and change. It rules over secrets and things hidden and is also allied with karmic energies.

USES: 1. Evolving your magickal ideas.

2. Use when dealing with investments or speculation.

3. Use for finding lost things.

4. To promote good mental health in healing.

Another powerful rune of protection, EOLH was often carved into weapons for victory and safety during battle. As its shape is the one we stand in when we invoke the gods or draw down energy from the heavens, it is also seen as the connecting bridge between gods and men.

USES: 1. Protection from enemies.

2. Protection from evil.

3. Promotes friendships.

4. Strengthens luck and the life force.

SIGEL is the rune of the will. It is that spiritual energy which guides all true seekers. A rune of success.

USES: 1. Victory, success.

2. Used for healing.

3. Used when strength and self-confidence are needed.

This is the great rune of victory and symbolizes kings and leaders of men. TIR is the rune of "might for right" and as such is valuable in a runescript when you have been unfairly denied something or have been falsely accused. It is indicative of the fighting spirit, of trial by combat and fearlessness. It is the primary masculine rune.

USES:
1. Victory.

2. Use whenever competition is a factor.

3. Good for health—encourages quick recuperation.

4. In love matters, TIR is used to symbolize the ardent male.

BEORC is the rune of the Great Mother and as such is the primary rune of fertility. It also conceals and protects and rules over all protective enclosures, such as houses or temple areas. It is very good to use in a runescript for the peace, projection and harmony of a household. In a runescript, it represents a very feminine and nurturing female type.

USES:
1. Fertility.

2. Protection.

3. Family matters.

4. To bring ideas to fruition.

5. To represent a certain type of female in the runescript.

This is a rune of abrupt changes and is good for initiating bold new ventures. Use EHWAZ after the "subject" runes in your runescript to facilitate change.

USES: 1. Brings change swiftly.

2. Ensures safe travel.

MANNAZ is the symbol of mankind as a whole and is often used when assistance from others is needed. It also symbolizes the powers of the rational mind.

USES: 1. To gain the assistance of others.

2. Increase in memory and mental powers.

LAGAZ is a rune of intuition and imagination. It is also a feminine rune, but unlike BEORC, it represents a strong and assertive female type.

USES: 1. Use to contact your intuitive faculties.

2. Increase in vitality and the life force (especially in women).

3. Helps to gather in energies for use by the will.

ᛝ ING represents the male consort of the Earth Mother and as such is also a symbol of fertility. It is often used in the final position of the runescript to indicate a successful outcome. It is a very positive rune.

USES: 1. Fertility.

2. To release energy suddenly.

3. To bring something to a satisfactory end.

4. To "fix" the outcome of your runescript so that the benefits indicated therein do not drain away.

ᛞ DAEG is the rune of the New Day. It symbolizes the feelings embodied in the expression "Today is the first day of the rest of your life." It is particularly good for fresh starts in any endeavor.

USES: 1. Good for financial increase.

2. To change an attitude, either yours or someone else's.

3. New beginnings.

◇ OTHEL signifies possessions or ancestral lands and characteristics. This rune encourages a down-to-Earth attitude of life.

USES: 1. When paired with FEHU, good for monetary gains.

2. Use wherever the health of the elderly is the issue.

3. Protection of possessions.

THE PRINCIPLES
OF RUNE MAGICK

Runes are pictorial representations of natural forces. It is the manipulation of these natural forces that we will be discussing in this section. This manipulation is commonly called *magick* and is a very misunderstood science indeed.

Magick means different things to different people. To most who spell it "magic" without the "k," it is associated with rabbits popping out of hats and children's parties. Thanks to the influence of foreign religions on the European cultures, a thing that was taken very seriously by our ancestors is today merely considered to be fit for the amusement of children, something done by illusionists to entertain us. It is an unreal thing based on tricks and showmanship.

On the other hand, magick (spelled with a "k" to distinguish it from dime store charades) does not rely on tricks. It works instead through formulae and ritual. This type of magick is not an extinct form of superstition—it is a workable system.

Why does magick work? It works because you *believe* it works. It doesn't just happen, however. You must *make* it happen. The way you make it happen is through belief and understanding. You must have belief in yourself and in the operation, and you must understand the operation thoroughly.

Aleister Crowley wrote in *Magick in Theory & Practice*: "Magick is the Science and Art of causing Change to occur in conformity with Will," and anyone who has ever performed magick of any kind can attest to the truth of that statement. Magick is not "supernatural." It is a well-thought-out and self-willed scientific exercise in which the results are known before they actually happen. Through the use of rune symbols, color, ritual and the force of your mind, you can "program" your operation, much like you can program your computer, using related bits of information to "tell" the forces what needs doing, confident in the outcome.

Magick using runes works because, as we have already seen, each runic symbol represents a conceptual force. These symbols can be arranged in such a way that if they were to occur in a runecast they would foretell precisely the event that you wish to magickally cause. This pools their forces together, and through concentration and visualization, these forces can be magickally gathered and sent out into the world to work your will.

As you can see, belief is the key to success in any magickal operation. If you find the idea of universal runic forces to be ludicrous, then of course your magick won't work, no matter how skillfully you lay out your runes. You will find your magick becoming more effective as your understanding and confidence grows, and the key to that understanding is to be found in what I call the Principle of Oneness.

For years people have rejected the Pagan view that the Earth itself is a living organism just as an insect or a tree is a living organism. The Earth is just another collection of cells coming together to form a whole with those cells being rocks, trees, humans, plankton and everything else that Is. Each part is essential to the healthy functioning of the whole.

Science is just now beginning to understand the truth of this most ancient of concepts, but the people who used the runes knew and accepted this just as they knew and accepted magick. Their belief in this Oneness is vividly illustrated in this quote in *Rune Games* from the medieval philosopher Basilius Valentinus:

"The Earth is not a dead body but is inhabited by the spirit that is its life and soul. All created things draw their strength from this Earth spirit. This spirit is life; it is nourished by the stars and it gives nourishment to all living things it shelters in its womb."

We are one with everything that exists. Everything that Is was made by some higher

Force along the ordered lines of concrete physical laws. Along with all life, we partake of the communal Life Force, and as we partake, so can we interact. This interaction is magick.

The Life Force that is indigenous to our planet is our Creator's legacy to all living things. It cannot be owned, yet it belongs to all of us, and its power has been utilized by the knowledgeable since the dawn of man.

It is from this Source that the runic vibrations are drawn, and it is to this Source they return, bound together in a purposeful way by the magician. The more you meditate on and work with the runes, the easier it will be to feel this energy as a tangible force that you can mold according to your personal needs.

Notice that I said "needs" and not "whims" or "desires." Magick should not be used for petty desires. It can be, of course, but often you will have no luck with it. The key to the effectiveness of any operation is the sheer force of will the magician uses to charge the operation. Without a true need, it is often difficult to project the force needed to complete the work. The magician who will be evicted from his apartment if he does not come up with the rent is likely to be more successful with his money magick than the greedy businessman who wants to win the lottery!

If you truly believe that you can succeed, then there is no reason why you shouldn't. Magick may seem to be a blind faith enterprise at first, but the more successes you have, the more proof you will have of its efficacy. The laws of magick are the laws of cause and effect, and they work in the unseen world just the same as they do in the world of matter. Forget any preconceived notions you may have about magick being all mysterious and complicated. *It is a science for subtly changing your reality.* If you follow the rules, choose the correct runes, and have a genuine need and a belief in yourself, then your magick is sure to be a success.

TALISMANS

"Runes and charms are very practical formulae designed to produce definite results, such as getting a cow out of a bog."

—T.S. Eliot

Talisman, as defined by the *Random House Dictionary of the English Language* is: 1) A stone, ring, or other object, engraved with figures or characters supposed to possess occult powers and worn as an amulet or charm, 2) Any amulet or charm, 3) Anything whose presence exercises a remarkable or powerful influence on human feelings or actions.

This last definition is the crux of the matter. Talismans, when properly constructed, can exercise a remarkable influence over situations in your life. The power to do this does not come from the talismanic object itself but is entirely generated in the mind of the magician.

The runic talisman is your physical affirmation of a mental process which your will has set in motion. It is your *focus*. Through concentrating on the talisman, you can add more power to your magick. Through this concentration, the talisman becomes linked to the essential vibrations of the rune(s) involved, and the energies of natural runic forces and the applied will of the magician combine in the unseen worlds to cause the changes indicated by the talismanic layout.

The occult writer Dion Fortune once said that what we may consider "gods" are really artificial thought-forms built up over long periods of time by the worship of successive generations. Another writer, Hzhak Bentov, quoted in *Rune Games*, describes a hypothetical way in which a "god" might be created:

"He imagines a rock in the desert. This in-animate (yet not "dead" as we perceive it) object has a very low level of consciousness. Its threshold of conscious awareness is stimulated by contact with various small animals in the area who regard the rock as a safe haven against predators and the elements. When a human being who is sensitive to vibrations travels through this stretch of desert, he may sense something "different" about this particular stone. If he is of a faith which accepts the idea of animism and spirits, his awe of the stone may turn into homage, and then worship of it, thereby boosting the rock's embryonic con-sciousness even further and eventually the spirit in the stone is transformed into a god."

This of course takes a very long time. The making and charging of talismans can by no means be equated with creating a god-form, but it works on the very same principle and does not take nearly so long.

Before making an attempt at the construction of a talisman, you should make sure that you are very familiar with all of the runes involved and have a basic understanding of the occult principles you will be using.

When properly crafted, a talisman becomes a "living" entity, one that is preprogrammed by the magician for a certain purpose. The magician gives it a life and a "destiny" by infusing the talismanic base with the forces of the runes.

In the beginning, it is best to make talismans for yourself rather than for other people. As with divination, doing rune magick for other people is a great responsibility and one which can lead to negative karmic debts if done frivolously. Never do negative magick for other people or for yourself. You will need the practice of making talismans for yourself in order to build up your familiarity with the skills of concentration and visualization that are so necessary in satisfactory magickal work. When you feel truly comfortable with the magickal operations involved in the creation of talismans, then you will be ready to think about helping others with your skills.

The main requirement in the formulation of a talismanic object is that it contains the rune symbols which outline the purpose at hand and some signature or symbol representing the person or thing to be affected by the talismanic energies. The talisman should be designed in such a way that all of its symbols, front and back, are laid out in a harmonious and aesthetically pleasing fashion. *Magick is an orderly science, and the more orderly and harmonious its tools, the better the outcome.*

As with any other discipline, practice makes perfect, and it is good to spend some time developing the skills of carving and painting. The easier it is for you to do these things, the more energy you can devote to your visualization of the eventual outcome. This visualization is very important and should not be taken lightly. It is one of the most crucial aspects of your magickal work, second only to belief. It is also one of the most difficult, and spending a lot of time worrying about your craftsman ability will rob your operation of valuable energy.

Almost anything can become a runic talisman. A special "tine" can be fashioned to accept your magickal symbols. This tine is usually created from wood since it is easy to work, but it can also be made from stone, paper, metal or bone. The degree of skill you have as a craftsman should be the determining factor in the choice of material used. Someone who barely feels comfortable with pen and paper will surely get in over his or her head trying to engrave a sterling silver tine, probably having so much difficulty that his or her concentration will be thrown off completely, dooming the operation altogether. Stick with what you feel comfortable with—the material doesn't really matter; it's the intent that counts. Usually these specialized rune tines are for purely magickal purposes; they have no other function.

There are other types of rune talismans which do perform a function above and beyond the magickal. Ordinary everyday objects can be made into talismans as well. Runes can be etched into a knife blade, painted somewhere on your car, carved on door lintels or used as jewelry. Handsome rune plaques made from wood can be charged with a particular function and hung in the home or workplace, bringing the runic energies closer to you and helping to create and restore harmony in your space.

If you are constructing your tine from wood, use the table in the back of this book to choose a wood that is sympathetic to the operation at hand. This can greatly increase the efficacy of your magick.

In Figure 3, I have illustrated a few of the best shapes for your rune tine. These can be used as a guide for inventing your own shapes. The traditional forms are the thicker rectangular tine and the thin stave. The former can be constructed from wood you gather yourself, while the latter is usually made from a store-bought wood veneer.

The nice thing about wood veneers is that if you can find a hobby or hardware store which sells them you will usually have a wider selection of "magickally significant" woods to choose from than you are likely to find in the wild. The bad thing about them is their thickness. A bit more

Tine Shapes

Figure 3

care must be taken with their carving to ensure
that they do not split or break in half.

If you choose to harvest your wood from the
wild, do not forget to honor the tree from whence
it came. The best times to collect the wood for
talismans are dawn, twilight, and high noon. Go

to your chosen tree, quietly stand in front of it and compose your thoughts. Concentrate on your need and the purpose of the tine you are about to make, then circle the tree *nine* times (nine being an extremely potent magickal number) while saying something like this:

> *Hail to thee, O tree of Oak (or Ash or whatever)!*
> *I respectfully ask you for this branch.*
> *Into it send thy energy*
> *That it may aid me in my work*
> *All for the good!*

Repeat as many times as is necessary for you to make the nine rounds about the tree. Then proceed to cut off the branch that you want. It is good at this time to visualize the runes that are to be carved upon it if you have decided on them. This is not necessary but is helpful in both infusing your subconscious as well as the living wood with the runic energies involved.

Once you have completed your harvesting, always remember to thank the spirit of the tree for its generosity and good energy.

Now that you have your wood, the actual talismanic formulation can begin. As mentioned earlier, magick is a science based on ritual formulae. Our minds could perform the necessary magick without this ritual formulae, but the use of a formula acts as a focus for our energies and makes magick easier.

There are several aspects of talismanic construction in addition to a proper choice of runes which can be very helpful in giving your magick an extra boost. These aspects are:

Choice of a sympathetic wood;
Choice of a sympathetic color for the rune symbols;
Construction in the proper moon phase;
Construction on a sympathetic day of the week.

All of this information, and then some, can be found in the tables at the back of this book.

Once again, it must be stated that none of this embellishment is really necessary for a successful outcome, but it can certainly help. Use your intuition to find what works best for you. Your intuition, your "gut feeling," will aid you along your path far more than merely parroting my instructions. The ideas and methods in this book have been found useful by myself and others in our magickal workings. They may be useful for you as well, but if they are not, then by all means search your heart until you find something that is.

Runescripts

Runescripts are *groups of runes arranged in a straight line that indicate a certain outcome by their positioning.* A working knowledge of the magickal attributes of each rune and a little common

sense are all that is required for the effective construction of a runescript talisman.

By the time you have reached this point, you
should have that working knowledge and be well
able to compose logical combinations of runes
for yourself, but a few hints and examples will be
included here.

First of all, you might find Appendix II useful. Here you can see at a glance specific categories
and the runes that apply to them. From these
runes, you can easily choose which individual
ones are best suited to your purpose.

Runescripts are usually composed of three,
five, seven, or nine runes. Eleven and 13 are also
powerful magickal numbers, but it is usually un-
necessary to have that many runes on a talisman.
Try not to clutter your runescript. Get your idea
formulated and be concise in your choice of runes.
Don't overdo it. More is not necessarily better.

If you wish, you can choose the number of
runes in your runescript based on the purpose of
the talisman. This is yet another way you can
integrate harmonious influences into your talismanic construction. The number *three* is useful
for talismans involving growth or an increase of
some sort. *Five* is good for all operations involving protection, defense, and victory. *Seven* is the
best number for love magick, and *nine* is the
number of the Norns—of destiny.

Of course, you may use any number of runes
for your talisman. The important thing is to know
why you chose the specific runes involved. For

example, suppose you have been single for a long time and wish for a companion. You may choose to make a talisman to aid you in your search. You know that seven is the number for operations of love, so you must try to find seven runes which express for you the nature of your desire.

The two most important runes in any magickal runescript are the *first* rune and the *final* rune. The first rune says "This is how I want the operation to start," and the final rune says "This is how I want things to end up." The runes in between elaborate on the subject of the talisman. A talisman must start out right and end up right in order to be truly effective. Making a correct choice is not really something that can be taught in a fixed sense. It must be a very personal choice based on the needs and wants of the individual.

In the case of this love talisman, we will assume that you would like a change in your relationship status, and the sooner the better. Therefore, we might begin the runescript with

ᚾ , this being a rune of change, useful for bringing new situations into your life. The rune to follow it could be ᚲ , because it governs the passions and is a strengthening influence in any operation. Following ᚲ , you may choose to place ᚹ , which is indicative of your intense need for love as well as having the power to draw a lover to you. Next we should put ᚷ , being a sign of love and partnership, followed by ᛈ to push the issue. After those runes, you may wish to include ᚠ to indicate the happiness you hope to attain, ending up the runescript with ᚾ . ING will "seal in" the magick of the runes preceding it and will not allow the power you have raised to drain away. This will give you the completed runescript ᚢᚲᛉᚷᚹᛈᚾ .

A simple talisman to attain money could use the runes ᛞᚠᚾ . ᛞ signifies new beginnings and financial increase; ᚠ indicates the money itself; and ᚾ protects the possessions you will eventually receive.

This is the way runescripts are created. With a little imagination, you can formulate a runescript for any occasion that will be very helpful to you in solving problems and bringing about changes in your life.

Many books give examples of precreated runescripts, and as you can see, this one is no exception. However, it is always best to create them yourself for your specific needs. When you utilize a ready-made runescript from a book, you are divorcing yourself from the actual ordering of a set of runic forces for the job, and you are merely relying upon someone else's idea of how these forces should be put together.

This is why some precreated runescripts do not always appear to work as they were intended. They may have worked very well for the original creator, but they often lose something in the translation when used blindly by someone else. You may feel insecure in your ability to put together an effective runescript, but if you study the rune meanings and have a very clear picture of what it is you wish to achieve, you should be more than capable of creating a useful talisman for just about any occasion. Remember, it is the lack of confidence in ourselves and in the outcome of our magickal operations that causes failure. With confidence, success is certain.

Bindrunes

Another way runes can be utilized for talismanic purposes is in the form of bindrunes. The main difference between runescripts and bindrunes is that instead of being written in a straight line like runescripts, a bindrune is made up of *several runes superimposed upon one another in a harmonious fashion.* Notice I said "harmonious"—it is very important when formulating a bindrune to choose individual runes that look good when placed together.

This is why it is really recommended that you use five runes or less in your bindrune composition. To use more than five is to run the risk of having a bindrune so cluttered that you really cannot distinguish one rune from another.

Bindrunes must be aesthetically pleasing. In order to achieve this, they can be composed of runes facing whatever way that it takes to achieve a harmonious effect, even upside down. Some runes, such as WUNJO and FEHU, look very nice when placed back to back, forming a mirror image of themselves. The magickal nature of the bind-rune permits this, and even runes that appear reversed will act as though upright. Because of this, bindrunes are practically foolproof, and a lot more artistic license can be taken in their construction. Experiment with different runes to see which arrangement suits them best. After you finish your design, you will often find upon closer examination "hidden runes" formed by the intersections of the other runes in the design. It is fun to look for these, and they will nearly always be found to apply to the matter at hand. These are "bonuses" to be found in a good composition.

Bindrunes are ideal for the beginner because either they will work or they won't. As long as your rune choices are the correct ones, the talisman will work. If your runes are haphazardly put together, the talisman probably won't be effective, but you need not worry about any negativity rebounding on you as is often the case when you make a mistake with other forms of magick. Bindrunes are totally harmless in that regard as well as being highly effective. With a little practice, you will find it easy to create effective bindrune talismans.

Bindrunes take up much less space than runescripts and should be used whenever space is a problem or visual design is important. They are aesthetic designs which can often be openly displayed without anyone questioning their purpose or suspecting magickal intent. Bindrunes are especially good for talismans that will be worn as jewelry or will be out in the open where ordinary people can see them.

Even with their lenient methods of construction, bindrune talismans are no less serious or effective than the runescript talismans, and the same care and thought must be taken in their formulation.

It is always good to think very hard and meditate on the proper runes for the resolution of the matter in question. Be sure you truly understand the magickal purpose that you have in mind. If you truly understand your problem, then your choice of runes should reflect this and act swiftly to resolve it.

The *central* rune in your bindrune arrangement should be a powerful indicator of the subject you have in mind. Thus, in matters of love, it is good to use X, the rune of partnership, or ᛉ , the rune indicative of a need for love. To preserve or hold something requires | as a central rune. For protection, try using ʃ or Y . Try different combinations until you find one that "clicks," and always remember that you must find your own personal method of construction. Use these pages as a guide, but also utilize your intuitive faculties. When it comes to dealing with your personal life, your intuition will serve you far better than any book.

Good Luck

To Win the Love
of a Woman

Preserve a Love
Relationship

Prosperity

Protect Possessions

Completed Bindrunes

Figure 4

Figure 4 illustrates a few completed bind-runes and their meanings. Analyze them and look for the hidden runes while trying to understand why each rune was chosen for that particular bindrune. Studying the individual meanings of the runes in these precreated bindrunes can tell you much that is useful.

RITUAL CARVING
AND CONSECRATION

Although the title of this chapter speaks of ritual "carving," the same ritual formulae apply whether you carve, etch or paint the runes onto your talisman. Carving the runes into wood is the traditional method, and it can also be one of the trickiest. Practice and a good technique are very important. That's why before getting into the ritual part of talismanic construction some time should be spent discussing the proper way to carve.

Most woods can be carved with an ordinary X-ACTO® knife. The trick is to first carve the primary lines of the rune (Fig. 5A). Then carve a small horizontal line at the endpoints of the rune (5B). This defines your endpoints and helps to prevent accidentally carving beyond them. Figs. 5C, D, E, and F illustrate different aspects of the final finishing. In 5C, the dotted lines show where to make finishing cuts. They run parallel to the primary cut, and as seen in D, E and F, should be

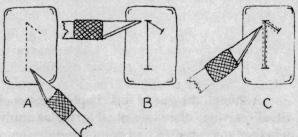

Steps in Carving

Figure 5

cut at a 45 degree angle to the center cut. The resulting sliver of wood can be easily popped out, giving your rune a nice uniform width and depth. This is a very effective method of carving and is easily mastered with practice.

You should (ideally) have an X-ACTO® knife or other carving instrument that is solely for the purpose of carving your talismans. This way the knife can absorb your personal energies and carving skill, thus aiding you well in any talismanic magick you might undertake. However, this may not always be desirable or possible, and the most important thing to remember about your knife is to keep a sharp blade in it! In carving, more injuries occur from blades that are past their prime than occur from blades that are razor sharp.

The first thing you will need is a quiet space with an altar or a work table that can remain relatively undisturbed. On this work surface, you should gather together all of the items necessary to your ritual. These items will vary according to personal need, but here is a recommended list for you to go by:

1. Your blank talisman. This should be complete and in its final form, except for the rune symbols you will be carving now.
2. The carving tool.
3. The coloring pigment.

4. A natural fiber cloth (black or the color appropriate to the operation) large enough in which to wrap the talisman.
5. Some natural twine or a leather thong long enough to wrap around the talisman nine times.
6. Candles.
7. Incense.
8. Salt.
9. Water.

You may also wish to include clothing or an altar cloth in the proper magickal colors. This is optional, as are items such as religious images. The purpose of ritual is to encourage a state of mind conducive to the magick at hand, and although all of the above are merely props, they are very effective in the right combinations for energizing a magickal space.

When you have all of the necessary objects on your table, you are ready to begin. Light your candles (if you are using them) and proceed to quiet your mind. Concentrate on the changes the talisman will work in your life. Imagine how your life will be when you achieve your goal—in other words, SEE yourself in that new job; SEE yourself with funds enough to pay your debts; SEE yourself in a happy, loving relationship. If you can see these things in your mind's eye, it will go a long way towards achieving them. If the talisman is for someone else, concentrate on the person for whom it was made and the effects it will have on his or her life. It is also good to inform the person of the time when you will be empowering the talisman so that s/he can sit quietly and concentrate on the operation as well. It is not necessary that s/he be present; in fact, unless s/he is well-versed in magick, it is best to have the person nowhere near you. However, having him or her concentrate on a successful outcome can be very helpful for all concerned. Additional energy never hurts!

Once you have the ritual outcome firmly in your mind, you may begin your carving.

The first thing you will do is carve the name of the person that the talisman is being created for or a symbol to represent him or her into the REVERSE side of the talismanic object. This is optional if the talisman will be worn or carried on a regular basis, but often the reinforcement of the name/symbol is helpful. Appendix I gives the runes and the modern English letter which they represent. Using this, any word can be transliterated into runic form, empowering it with the rune energies.

Next, you will set about carving your runescript or bindrune on the front of the talisman. This is a very important part of the ritual and should be attended to with great care. The process of carving and energizing runescripts and bindrunes is identical for both, but there are a couple of points which need to be brought up before the actual carving should begin.

If you refer back to Figure 3, you will notice that the two runescripts illustrated there are bordered top and bottom by horizontal lines. These are common in runescript talismans and are useful for linking the energies of the runes together into one amalgamated force. They also serve the practical purpose of providing a finite boundary for your vertical cuts, and this neatens up the runescript's appearance. These two lines should be the last things carved in the runescript to bind the runes together.

Each rune in the runescript must be carved and charged separately. This is also the case with bindrunes. When you formulate your bindrune, decide which rune should come first and in what order the others should follow. Then when you carve, carve and charge each rune in its proper order and in the completed final form, thus bringing the individual rune forces together into a concrete symbol of harmonious energy.

This charging involves intense concentration and visualization. When you carve each individual rune, chant its name and concentrate on its function in the talismanic layout. You should feel the rune force as a tangible thing, flowing out of your arm, into your knife and into the carved symbol itself. This is definitely a learned skill, and although some people are more naturally adept than others, it takes time to master, so you should not feel like your magick is doomed to failure if you do not succeed in arousing this energy your first few times.

When all of the runes have been carved into your talisman, it is time to apply the color. This should be done carefully. It is important to stay within the lines—don't be sloppy. Apply your color first to the side of the talisman bearing the name/symbol. While you color these runes, concentrate on the ability of the color to link the name runes with the magickal runescript on the front, and recite this formula or substitute one of your own:

> Odin and Freya, look upon this carving with
>   favor;
> Let the colors and symbols empower it
> And let this talisman be a successful one for
>   (name)!

As you apply the color, imagine that as it touches the rune symbols it unlocks and activates the power that you have sent into the wood during the carving phase. Feel the power thrumming in the wood as you concentrate on the purpose of the talisman. KNOW that the power is present, both in the wood and in your own mind. Feel the energy of it, then relax.

Next, take the talisman and carefully wrap it in the cloth, binding it nine times around with your cord. Nine was the most mystical number in the minds of the rune-using peoples and symbolizes the powers of the Norns—the forces of destiny. The reason we wrap up the talisman is to give it its own magickal "space" in which to retire from the light and develop its full energies. Concentrate on the wrapped talisman and "see" its power growing. Lay it in the center of your table and circle it nine times while speaking aloud the purpose of the talisman. This is a very important magickal step and binds your intention firmly to the talismanic object.

When you feel that enough energy has been raised, unbind the cord and slowly open up the cloth. This is your talisman's "birth time" when its energies are called forth into a finished existence.

Place your mouth close above the talisman, and using your maximum force of breath, breathe long and hard over it while visualizing your personal life force entering the object, animating it to work its magick. This process of "breathing life" into an object is one of the most ancient forms of sympathetic magick practiced by many different cultures all over the world. It is very common because it is very effective.

Using your right index finger (or a magickal implement such as a wand or athame, if you have one), tap three times upon the talisman. You may also use a bell, ringing it three times. This "gets the attention" of the spirit in the talisman and activates it to perform its work.

If you wish to strengthen this spirit even more, you may choose to give it a name. This name should in some way reflect the talisman's purpose, such as "Increase in Prosperity" or "Force of Love." This practice is a direct hearkening back to the names the ancients gave to their weapons, drinking horns, etc., to make them more effective in their given functions. Pass the talisman over the flame of a candle three times while speaking the name aloud. This infuses the talisman with the powers of Fire. Sprinkle it with Water and say "I give thee the name (name)." Pass it through the incense smoke, saying "I charge thee to thy purpose and infuse thee with the powers of Air." Then take your salt and sprinkle a few grains upon the talisman, saying "I purify thee with the element Earth and charge thee to thy purpose."

At this time, you should have a very clear picture in your mind of the talisman as a functioning entity and a clear understanding of the work it will perform in the formative spheres. This image can be actualized by composing a concise summary in which all of the aspects of the talisman's usefulness should be stated aloud, reinforcing the concepts in your mind and informing the powers that be of your magickal intention. Be sure to also state the length of time the talisman is to work. If you are not sure, then say "until its work is completed" or something to that effect.

When you have decided what you will say, stand over the talisman with your arms upraised and speak your magick aloud. Visualize the gods and forces hearkening to it, pleased with your intention and ready to lend their powers, if need be. When you feel that enough energy has been raised, thank the forces for their attendance and proclaim the ritual closed.

Now the talisman is fully charged and can be

placed where it is to exercise its influence or given to the person for whom it was made.

Some talismans, such as the ones used as jewelry or carved upon knives, have no "expiration date" per se, and as long as they were properly charged the first time, they need never be ritually charged again. There is no reason why they cannot be, however, and if you ever feel the need to charge the item again, by all means do so.

Other talismans, such as the ones to attract money or love, must be ritually "released" from service once their function has been fulfilled. This is a simple procedure and can be done according to personal preference. The most common ways of releasing the residual energy are by burning the wood tine or burying it in the ground, allowing any remaining energy to be dissipated back into the Earth. If you wish to reuse the talisman blank, then the runes may merely be whittled from its surface and the resulting shavings burned or buried in the Earth. This should be done in whatever way your intuition guides you and with all of the ceremony you can invent.

In this section, I have tried to give you a basic idea of the elements a proper talismanic charging ritual should contain. If you do not care for any part of this ritual, leave it out; by the same token, if you wish to add something to it, do so, but keep in mind what was said earlier about thoroughly understanding why you are making these alterations. Items should never be added or deleted without a good reason, but if this is the case, then it is perfectly acceptable to change your ritual accordingly.

Done properly, talismanic magick is one of the most effective magickal operations you can perform. Always know WHY you are doing your magick, always do it for the right reasons, always do it with care and respect, and you won't go wrong.

Good luck in your runic studies. The information in this book is but a fraction of what can be learned. Always be open to receive new ideas and knowledge, and may Odin and Freya bless and guide you.

So mote it be!

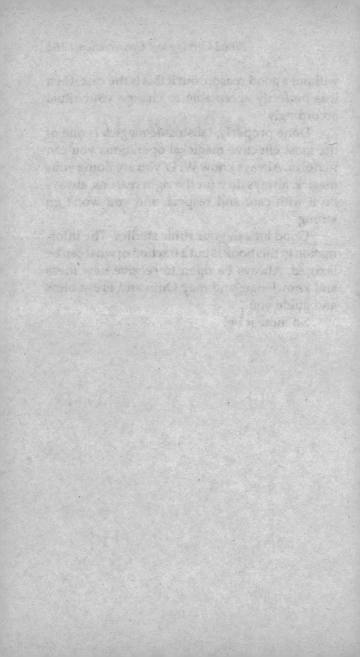

APPENDIX I

A: ᚠ   O: ◊

B: ᛒ   P: ᚲ

C: ᚲ   Q: ᚲ

D: ᛞ   R: ᚱ

E: ᛗ   S: ᛋ

F: ᚠ   T: ↑

G: ᚷ   U: ᚢ

H: ᚺ   V: ᚢ or ᚦ

I: | or ᛋ   W: ᚦ

J: | or ᛉ   X: ᚲᛋ (KS)

K: ᚲ   Y: ᛉ

L: ᚱ   Z: ᛋ or ᛯ

M: ᛗ   TH: ᚦ

N: ᛏ   NG: ᚷ

APPENDIX II

Easy Rune Reference

Money, Possessions: ᚠ ᛗ ᛟ

Love: ᚠ ᚦ ᚲ ᚷ ᚹ ᛉ ᛁ ᛏ ᛒ ᛟ

Protection: ᚹ ᚢ ᛉ ᛁ ᛃ ᛇ ᛒ

New Beginnings: ᚠ ᚲ ᛗ

Victory: ᚦ ᛋ ᛏ

Health and Well-Being: ᚢ ᚲ ᛈ ᛋ ᛏ ᛃ ᛚ ᛟ

Luck: ᚹ ᚢ ᛇ

Fertility: ᛜ ᛒ ᛟ

Travel: ᚱ ᛖ

Communications and Legal Matters:
ᚨ ᚱ ᛜ

APPENDIX III

Colors

GREEN: Healing, prosperity, luck, fertility

BROWN: Protection of physical objects, magick for animals

YELLOW: Communications, legalities, attraction

ORANGE: Attraction, luck

RED: Sexual love, protection, courage, vital health

BLUE: Healing, peace

PURPLE: Power, prosperity, healing

WHITE: Protection, purity, truth

BLACK: Absorption and destruction of negativity

APPENDIX IV

The Four Compass Points—Their Use In Magick

NORTH (Earth): Growth, material gain, employment, prosperity, stability and fertility. The colors green and brown.

EAST (Air): The mind, intuitive and psychic work, all matters of communication and legalities. The color yellow.

SOUTH (Fire): Purification, combat, sex magick, healing. The color red.

WEST (Water): Emotions, matters of love, intuitive work, dreams and general happiness. The color blue.

APPENDIX V

Days of the Week

Day	God/Goddess	Works For
Sunday	Baldur	Healing, Family
Monday	Freya	Divination, Love
Tuesday	Tir	Protection, Victory
Wed.	Odin	Healing, Knowledge
Thursday	Thor	Wealth, Prosperity
Friday	Frigga	Love, Fertility
Saturday	The Norns	Fate, Destiny, Luck

APPENDIX VI

The Moon

Use the New Moon for all operations involving new beginnings and for initiating your magickal workings.

Use the time from the first quarter to the Full Moon for all operations of growth, such as those for love, prosperity, luck and healing. (This healing would be a MENDING type such as healing surgical scars or knitting a broken bone.)

Use the Full Moon to culminate any growth-type magick you may have in the works.

Use the time from the third quarter to the New Moon for all magick involving protection, banishing, disintegration of relationships and all healing that has to do with eradicating something (such as shrinking a cancerous tumor or getting rid of a virus).

NOTE: As with any other supplementary information, it is not necessary to exactly follow these guidelines. When magick is needed, it is needed, and sometimes you may not be able to wait for the proper Moon phase. In this case, try to at least work on the proper day of the week for your needs. Keep in mind these things: Waxing—growth, increase; Waning—stagnation, decrease.

The influences of the New and Full Moons extend three days before and three days after the actual astronomical moments of Newness and Fullness.

APPENDIX VII

Magickal Properties Of Trees

APPLE: Love, fertility
ASH: Protection
ASPEN: Protection
BIRCH: Protection, fertility, new beginnings
CEDAR: Prosperity
ELDER: Healing, protection, prosperity
ELM: Protection
JUNIPER: Protection
MAPLE: Love
OAK: Healing, prosperity
PINE: Healing, prosperity, fertility
ROWAN: Protection
WALNUT: Healing, protection
WILLOW: Healing, protection, love
YEW: Protection

SUGGESTED
READING LIST

Blum, Ralph. *The Book of Runes*. New York: St. Martin's Press, Inc., 1982.

Branston, Brian. *The Lost Gods of England*. New York: Thames & Hudson, 1957.

Cunningham, Scott. *Earth Power: Techniques of Natural Magic*. St. Paul, MN: Llewellyn Publications, 1984.

Howard, Michael. *The Runes*. Wellingborough, Northamptonshire, England: Aquarian Press, 1980.

Osborne, Marijane and Stella Longland. *Rune Games*. Boston: Routledge & Kegan Paul, Ltd., 1982.

Thorsson, Edred. *Futhark: A Handbook of Rune Magick*. York Beach, ME: Samuel Weiser, Inc., 1984.

Willis, Tony. *The Runic Workbook: Understanding & Using the Power of Runes*. Wellingborough, Northamptonshire, England: Aquarian Press, 1986.

☽ Order LLewellyn Books today!

Llewellyn publishes hundreds of books on your favorite subjects! To get these exciting books, including the ones on the following pages, check your local bookstore or order them directly from Llewellyn.

ORDER BY PHONE
- Call toll-free within the U.S. and Canada, 1-877-NEW-WRLD
- In Minnesota, call (651) 291-1970
- We accept VISA, MasterCard, and American Express

ORDER BY MAIL
- Send the full price of your order (MN residents add 7% sales tax) in U.S. funds, plus postage & handling to:

  Llewellyn Worldwide
  P.O. Box 64383, Dept. L593-3
  St. Paul, MN 55164–0383, U.S.A.

POSTAGE & HANDLING
(For the U.S., Canada, and Mexico)
- $4.00 for orders $15.00 and under
- $5.00 for orders over $15.00
- No charge for orders over $100.00

We ship UPS in the continental United States. We ship standard mail to P.O. boxes. Orders shipped to Alaska, Hawaii, The Virgin Islands, and Puerto Rico are sent first-class mail. Orders shipped to Canada and Mexico are sent surface mail.

International orders: Airmail—add freight equal to price of each book to the total price of order, plus $5.00 for each non-book item (audio tapes, etc.).

Surface mail—Add $1.00 per item.

Allow 2 weeks for delivery on all orders.
Postage and handling rates subject to change.

DISCOUNTS
We offer a 20% discount to group leaders or agents. You must order a minimum of 5 copies of the same book to get our special quantity price.

FREE CATALOG
Get a free copy of our color catalog, *New Worlds of Mind and Spirit*. Subscribe for just $10.00 in the United States and Canada ($30.00 overseas, airmail).

Visit our web site at www.llewellyn.com for more information.

WITCHES RUNES
Cards created and illustrated by Nigel Jackson
Rune Mysteries by Nigel Jackson And Silver Ravenwolf

The snow-covered peaks, misty heaths, dark woods, and
storm-wracked seas of the Northern
World were the cradle of a remarkable
and bold mysticism whose essence is
concentrated in the runes. The runes
are a method of communicating with
divinity—the god/goddess within
each of us who embodies our pure con-
sciousness and inward spirituality.

The Witches Runes cards are rich in
beautiful imagery; along with the
accompanying book *Rune Mysteries*, they are a shortcut
to the esoteric rune system. Here, old American
witchcraft and European practices meld into a contemporary evolution of the Northern magickal lore. This system is of immediate and practical use in divination,
magick, and self-development. Even a little experience in
casting the Witches Runes cards will soon convince you
of the uncanny accuracy of their messages.

The cards' images were subtly constructed to contain
symbolic significance at a number of levels. This visual
"unfolding" of each rune's inner mysteries within each
card enables you to hear their oracular voices with
greater clarity than was ever before possible except at
the most advanced degrees of runic knowledge.

1-56718-553-3, Boxed set:
Book: Rune Mysteries, 6 x 9, 256 pp., illus., softcover
Deck: 24 full-color cards $29.95

NORTHERN MYSTERIES & MAGICK
Runes & Feminine Powers
Freya Aswynn

A classic contribution to rune lore . . .

The runes are more than an ancient
alphabet. They comprise a powerful
system of divination and a path to the
subconscious forces operating in your
life. *Northern Mysteries & Magick* is is the
first book of its kind to offer an extensive presentation of rune concepts,
mythology, and magickal applications
inspired by Dutch/Friesian traditional
lore.

Discover how the feminine Mysteries of the North are
represented in the runes, and how each of the major
deities of Northern Europe still live in the collective con-
sciousness of people of Northern European descent.
Chapters on runic divination and magick introduce the
use of runes in counseling and healing.

- Provides a balanced view of Norse mythology,
  emphasizing the feminine mysteries and the
  function of the Northern priestesses
- Includes a bookmark of the runes

1-56718-047-7
6 x 9, 288 pp., appendix, bibliog., index $14.95

THE RITES OF ODIN
Ed Fitch

The ancient Northern Europeans knew a
rough magic drawn from the grandeur of
vast mountains and deep forests, of
rolling oceans and thundering storms.
Their rites and beliefs sustained the
Vikings, accompanying them to the New
World and to the Steppes of Central Asia.
Now, for the first time, this magic system
is brought compellingly into the present
by author Ed Fitch.

This is a complete source volume on Odinism. It
stresses the ancient values as well as the magic and myth
of this way of life. The author researched his material in
Scandinavia and Germany, and drew from anthropological and historical sources in Eastern and Central Europe.

A full cycle of ritual is provided, with rites of passage,
magical spells, divination techniques, and three sets of
seasonal rituals: solitary, group and family. *The Rites of
Odin* also contains extensive "how-to" sections on plan-
ning and conducting Odinist ceremonies, including
preparation of ceremonial implements and the setting up
of ritual areas. Each section is designed to stand alone for
easier reading and for quick reference. A bibliography is
provided for those who wish to pursue the historical and
anthropological roots of Odinism further.

0–87542–224–1, 360 pp., 6 x 9, illus., softcover $17.95

NORSE MAGIC
D. J. Conway

The Norse: adventurous Viking wanderers, daring warriors, worshippers of the Aesir and the Vanir. Like the Celtic tribes, the Northmen had strong ties with the Earth and Elements, the Gods and the "little people."

Norse Magic is an active magic, only for participants, not bystanders. It is a magic of pride in oneself and the courage to face whatever comes. It interests those who believe in shaping their own future, those who believe that practicing spellwork is preferable to sitting around passively waiting for changes to come.

The book leads the beginner step by step through the spells. The in-depth discussion of Norse deities and the Norse way of life and worship set the intermediate student on the path to developing his or her own active rituals. *Norse Magic* is a compelling and easy-to-read introduction to the Norse religion and Teutonic mythology. The magical techniques are refreshingly direct and simple, with a strong feminine and goddess orientation.

0-87542-137-7, 240 pp., mass market, illus.   **$5.99**

MAGICAL I CHING

J.H. Brennan

It's the oldest book in the world . . . yet scholars disagree about its age. It has been consulted by millions in the Orient . . . yet no more than a handful have ever read it all. It is revered for its wisdom . . . yet it is used to tell fortunes.

Using coins, yarrow stalks, or even a computer, you can cast fortunes using six-lined figures known as hexagrams. This wholly new translation of the ancient Chinese *I Ching* helps you interpret the hexagrams, whose meanings continue to be useful throughout the ages, providing profound and strikingly accurate divinations.

More than a divination tool, the *I Ching* also has links with the Astral Plane and the Spirit World. Use it in ritual and pathworking, as an astral doorway or a spirit guide. Although there are many versions of the *I Ching* on the market, this is the first to delve into the magical techniques that underlie the oracle.

1-56718-087-6, 264 pp., 7 ½ x 9 ⅛ $14.95

TRUE MAGICK
A Beginner's Guide
Amber K

True Magick can change your life. With magick's aid, you can have vibrant health, prosperity or a new career. You can enhance your relationships or bring new ones into your life. With magick, you can reach deep inside yourself to find confidence, courage, tranquility, faith, compassion, understanding or humor. If you're curious about magick, you will find answers in this book.

Amber K, a High Priestess of the Wiccan religion and experienced practitioner of magick, explains not only the history and lore of magick, but also its major varieties in the world today. And if you want to practice magick, then this book will start you on the path.

0-87542-003-6, 272 pp., mass market, illus.   **$5.99**